"I've enjoyed working with the team at PassiveInvesting.com for several years. Passive investing works for me in so many ways, like the cash flow, equity growth, and can't forget the tax savings. It is a must for any serious real estate investor that doesn't want to have to worry about day-to-day management."

—Larry Correll, full-time passive real estate investor

"The PassiveInvesting.com team has written the most comprehensive and immersive apartment syndication book for investors. An easy-to-understand and practical guide, this is a must-read for anyone considering investing in apartments. I've experienced PassiveInvesting.com's proven strategies from day one and couldn't be happier for Dan and Danny to share their wealth of knowledge and experience with the world."

—Ryan McKenna, CEO and Founder, McKenna Capital

"Dan and Danny are uniquely positioned to help other real estate investors be successful in apartment syndication. Their passion for the syndication industry, combined with their understanding of the best business practices and effective marketing, gives them the knowledge needed to run a syndication business and to run it so that it is effective and financially successful. This book will also give you valuable tools to be a successful apartment syndicator."

—Joe Fairless, Founder of Best Ever Commercial Real Estate

"What an incredible resource! In this book, Danny and Dan did an extraordinary job outlining our exciting apartment syndication business. They are a world-class team in multifamily syndication and operations.

This valuable resource will give you the understanding and confidence to invest passively, or even actively, in this safe and lucrative asset class."

—Rod Khleif, host of the podcast
Lifetime Cash Flow through Real Estate Investing

"I've known and worked with Dan and Danny for over three years. During that time, I've been an investor, partner, and friend. I've come to know each of them professionally but also personally. We have worked on more than thirty projects together, totaling over $1 billion. One of the challenges in life is finding the right tribe, the right group that can take you to the next level. These people need to resonate with your principles, your goals, and your future. I'm fortunate to call this trio from PassiveInvesting.com part of my tribe. Not only have they helped me to reach my next level, but I've watched as they've helped thousands of others do the same, not only through investments but through sharing their knowledge. I'm confident that this book will help you on your journey."

—Chris Larsen, Founder, Next-Level Income

"Dan and Danny have a true wealth of knowledge to impart to those wise enough to take notes. If you own a syndication business or are thinking of starting one, the information within this book is not just theory, as the team at PassiveInvesting.com are active and in the trenches in the syndication space. Be sure to ask Dan about the marching-band marketing idea when he speaks. Classic!"

—Michael Blank, author of
Financial Freedom with Real Estate Investing

"Having seized the opportunity to participate in most of the PassiveInvesting.com syndications, we can easily vouch for the materials found in this book as being bonafide and generating results. Dan and Danny have taken their knowledge, gained through extremely hard work and diligent research in this real estate investing arena, and generously shared it with us and countless others. These rock-solid investing procedures and thorough implementation of the plan have generated incredible growth in our portfolio. We know this information can deliver incredible success. Happy investing!"

—Wyman and Janice Shull, passive real estate investors

"I have been a full-time real estate investor for over two decades but never fully understood apartment syndication until meeting Danny and Dan a few years ago. Since then, I have not only invested passively in over twenty different syndications but have done my own syndication as well. This would not have been possible without the knowledge and guidance given to me by these three guys. If you are interested in learning about apartment syndication from individuals who don't just talk the talk but who truly walk the walk, this book is for you!"

—Kelli Garrett, Managing Partner, Rehab Wallet

"In this five-star book, the authors demystify the art of apartment syndication. Whether you are a seasoned syndicator or an inquisitive beginner in passive investing, this book will give you the tools and fundamentals to actually run a successful real estate investing business. Real estate is not a get-rich-quick scheme, but with the knowledge in this book, it is a get-rich-for-sure playbook that will also show you there is more to success than just money."

—Yonah Weiss, cost-segregation expert,
host of the podcast *Weiss Advice*

"I've known Dan and Danny since they started their syndication business, PassiveInvesting.com, and I have always admired their work ethic and ingenuity. As an investor with PassiveInvesting.com, I appreciate their professional communication and polished approach to everything they do."

—Rob Beardsley, Founder, Lone Star Capital

Apartment Syndication

Apartment Syndication

Syndication

The Ultimate Guide for the Active or Passive Investor

Dan Handford
Danny Randazzo

Brandon Abbott

Acknowledgements

We'd like to thank the people who contributed to the creation of this book and to the success of PassiveInvesting.com and Multifamily Investor Nation:

Brandon Abbott, one of our founders, whose knowledge, insight, and hard work helped make PassiveInvesting.com a success, and whose contributions to this book have been invaluable. Brandon retired from PassiveInvesting.com in 2022, and we wish him and his family all the best.

Melissa Broom, who creates all our graphics and visual materials (inside and outside of the book) and designed our book cover.

And of course, to our families for their ongoing love and support.

Contents

Foreword

As a Master Coach and Business Strategist, I've dedicated over 30,000 hours to working with business owners, entrepreneurs, and real estate investors all over the world, to help them build incredible wealth, achieve success, and create an extraordinary quality of life for themselves and their families. I'm passionate about helping people realize their potential and live the life of their dreams. I'm always amazed when I meet clients who are extremely driven to be their best, and who surround themselves with others who want to live an extraordinary life.

Five years ago, I started coaching a new student who immediately pinged my radar as one to watch. He was passionate, driven, and showed up with energy and dedication in every aspect of his life: from his family to the way he approached personal growth, and especially his journey as a real estate investor.

That standout student was Danny Randazzo, and shortly after we met, he partnered up with another amazing individual, Dan Handford, to form a real dynamic duo. As they began working together, they started to achieve some phenomenal success.

Dan and Danny have diverse skill sets, but they also have a unified mindset and what I call *heartset* as well. Dan is outstanding with relationships and is a capital-raising phenom. Danny is a true financial wizard and very detail oriented, which is a huge part of their success. They share a powerful philosophy about operating their business with transparency and integrity, but most of all, they are all heart-driven, mission-focused people. They complement each other so well that they create a positive, dynamic cycle that propels them toward success.

Over the years, I've had a front-row seat to watch them grow in leaps and bounds. Not only have I had the pleasure to coach them from time to time, but also to share the stage at industry conferences and online summits. Being with them in person and seeing their true character shine through is truly amazing. I've also been so impressed and had so much confidence in their ability to perform in all facets of finding and investing in great opportunities, that I have personally invested with them on multiple occasions and continue to send new investors their way regularly!

The group at PassiveInvesting.com has rapidly grown to a dominant force in the industry. They have developed a proven methodology for growing an apartment syndication business. It's almost like they've got it down to a science.

I'm going to tell you a secret—it isn't science. It's alchemy. Dan and Danny have discovered how to create a business that's greater than the sum of its parts. It's all based on their belief that they aren't in the real estate business at all. They're in the relationship business. They know how to attract and build connections with like-minded, passionate people.

They understand that all of us—coaches, mentors, and investors— are better together. They've left no stone unturned in their own journey, and they freely offer up all their learning to others. They do the due diligence themselves. They plug investors into outstanding opportunities where they know their capital is preserved so they can sleep at night, but they can also have confidence that a tremendous upside is coming. Above all, they have developed and polished a reliable, repeatable, scalable system that develops not just businesses, but communities.

I love how they're willing to pull back the curtain for real people and real families. They truly understand what the average American is facing when deciding what asset class to put their money into. They want people to know what to do, what not to do, how it works, and why it works.

This book unpacks their methods so that anyone, whether they're new to real estate investing or an expert themselves, can gain a clear understanding and take their learning to a new level. Readers who want to become active investors will discover what it takes to roll up their sleeves and get after it. Those who want to put their capital to work passively can become knowledgeable about this opportunity and let Dan and Danny do the heavy lifting.

After all, learning information is great, but the essential thing is to put your knowledge to work. I think that's why the PassiveInvesting. com team has been able to build such a strong community nationally and even internationally. They teach the same information that they apply every day in their own business. They live their best and fullest life by bringing forward this blueprint for success for everyone to discover and apply in their own life.

If you're reading this book, you owe it to yourself to read it cover to cover and soak it up. When you start to apply the science, you can find the alchemy for yourself and begin to move even closer toward the wealth and freedom you truly deserve.

—Trevor McGregor,
Real Estate Investor
Master Platinum Coach
Business Strategist

Introduction

What is apartment syndication? We believe it's the single best investment opportunity you can find, for both passive income and long-term growth of your portfolio. That's why we do it.

In the simplest terms, apartment syndication is when a group of investors (a syndication) purchases a multifamily apartment complex and operates it for profit to split among the participants. What's not so simple is…the rest of it. It's a complex business model that, like all investments, carries risk. Passive investors need to understand how the business works (and how syndications *should* work) so they can make informed decisions about where to place their capital. Those who want to become active investors and operate their own business need to know where to start, what to do, and how to grow their skills.

That's why we wrote this book—for the active or passive investor.

If you're reading this book, then you must have some curiosity about real estate investing, specifically multifamily real estate investing. Investors in today's economic climate look for options beyond Wall Street, and real estate is a great way to round out a portfolio. When you own a physical asset, you actually have some control over how it performs, and during market cycles apartment communities typically outperform alternative investments.

Perhaps you have a healthy nest egg, but your returns are stagnant and you're concerned that your long-term savings aren't working as hard as they should be. Perhaps you're looking at the volatility of the stock market and you aren't a fan of roller coasters. Perhaps you already have some real estate investments and want to level up. Passive investing in multifamily syndications can be a great path to take care of your family and your future, as it is a great generational wealth-building tool.

On the other hand, maybe you don't have much of a nest egg yet, and your goal is to grow it. Maybe you have kids to put through college but you still want to retire (and preferably retire early). You're looking for financial freedom. Learning to organize and operate your own multifamily syndication business could be your ticket to that new life.

Wherever you're coming from and wherever you're trying to go, there's a key feature of apartment syndication that will help you get there: passive cash flow. Your investment in a healthy multifamily asset has the potential to generate reliable income for you, month after month, with a recession-proof asset to back it up. After all, in good economic times or bad, everybody needs a roof over their head.

While the individual components of multifamily real estate investing aren't difficult to understand or execute, there are a lot of components which make it complex! Learning all of these pieces of the apartment syndication puzzle can be overwhelming and confusing. This book offers you a comprehensive guide to navigate this valuable opportunity.

What You'll Learn

Everyone has a different style of learning. Our 40,000+ members at the *Multifamily Investor Nation* learn a lot from our weekly webinars and podcasts, but many of them have asked us for a book so they can study at their own pace, look back at topics easily, and have a reference guide with the information they need all in one place. That's our goal with this book.

First, we'll introduce you to the basics of apartment syndication as a business model, and the foundational knowledge you need to understand in order to be successful as a passive investor or an active operator. That includes the different paths you can follow to get started and grow your involvement, the terminology you should master, and the type of team a reliable operator needs to build. We'll cover the benefits of multifamily investing, alongside the challenges you may face when entering the industry. We'll also teach you how successful operators raise the kind of capital they need to purchase a 50, 60, or 100 million dollar asset, and how operators and passive investors receive their profits.

Next, we'll examine the anatomy of a multifamily acquisition. You'll learn how to set your investing criteria and find the right deals in the right markets for you and your future passive investors. You'll learn how multifamily deals are structured so you can set up your syndication properly, or for you to assess when a deal is solid or too good to be true. We'll teach you how operators can find and work with the best lender for any given deal. We'll also walk you through the acquisition process from initial bid to closing day.

Finally, you'll learn the fundamentals of operating an asset. That includes adding value to your physical property and working with a property manager, as well as financial and tax strategies you can use to maximize the benefits of your investment.

Who We Are

We're a team of professional real estate investors who operate multifamily assets in some of the fastest-growing real estate markets in the US and the managing partners of PassiveInvesting.com. We currently manage a portfolio of 47 properties valued at over $1.4 billion. We believe so strongly in the potential of this business model that we devote a great deal of time and energy to educating potential investors and future operators through our training platform, the *Multifamily Investor Nation*.

Dan Handford: I'm a serial entrepreneur, having grown multiple seven-figure businesses from scratch with combined annual budgets in excess of $10 million. I'm the founder of the *Multifamily Investor Nation*—I'm the business and marketing guy.

Danny Randazzo: I'm a financial consultant who has advised multi-billion dollar companies in growing revenue, increasing profits, and enhancing their use of technology. I'm a national speaker and the coauthor of *The Roadmap to Financial Success*, as well as the *Wealth Lessons for Kids* series of children's books. I'm the finance guy.

Brandon Abbott: I'm a top professional in the residential and commercial insurance industry, with over 15 years' experience in the real estate and construction fields and over 10 years as a real estate investor. I'm the acquisitions guy.

Nice to "meet" you. We're glad you're here. In the following chapters, we'll share our thoughts together when we talk about high-level concepts and overall business philosophy. For specialized information, we'll each weigh in on our personal areas of expertise. We want you to feel confident that you're getting your information straight from the source.

All Meat, No Bun

We have a website and a YouTube channel, but we're not "influencers" or lifestyle gurus. We're not going to hand you a bunch of vague platitudes about success mindset and visualization. You won't find any half-baked lists of to-dos with no context that wind up leading nowhere, and this book isn't a teaser that gives you half the story and persuades you to pay for the real knowledge.

This is the real knowledge. We have no paid coaching program to sell you.

We're giving you a comprehensive view of how the apartment syndication business works from the inside out. You'll know where your money is going and where your profits come from, and you'll have actionable advice every step of the way. For passive investors, it's an incredible opportunity as long as you find the right team to work with. For operators, it's not a part-time, low-effort gig. It's a grind—a very lucrative grind. We think it's worth it.

We've worked with thousands of investors who have found exponential wealth and life-changing opportunities in this business. To see that kind of success yourself, you need to thoroughly understand the basics. So let's get started.

Part 1

Apartment Syndication: What Is It, and How Does It Work?

If you are new to apartment syndication, we recommend that you spend some time absorbing the material in Part 1. It will introduce you, whether a passive investor or an aspiring syndicator, to the foundational concepts of how the business works, important terms you need to know, why it's a powerful investment opportunity, and some of the best practices that distinguish reliable, successful operating groups from struggling or over-extended operators.

In this section, you'll learn:

- Chapter 1: The Fundamentals of the Apartment Syndication Business
  - Identifying the elements of a syndication deal
  - How investors get paid
  - Paths to success for operators
  - How operators get paid
  - Industry-specific terminology

- Chapter 2: Why Invest in Large Apartments?
  - What makes multifamily investing so secure
  - The tax benefits of multifamily investments
  - How to get started with passive investing

- Chapter 3: Finding Investors
  - Why strong relationships with your investors are so important
  - Options for working with institutional investors

- Chapter 4: Five Steps to Successful Investor Relations
  - Building strong and trustworthy relationships with potential investors
  - Transparency and communication about investment opportunities
  - Organized, diligent, and timely execution of deal documents
  - Accountability in reporting and distributing returns
  - Cultivating a growing referral network

Chapter 1

Fundamentals of the Apartment Syndication Business

Learning the business of apartment syndication is a lot like learning a foreign language. On the one hand, you need to know vocabulary and grammatical structure so you understand what people are talking about and can carry on an intelligent conversation. On the other hand, you need to understand certain things about the culture so you can connect with people and avoid sticking out like a sore thumb.

In the business of multifamily, you need to grasp the terminology and the deal structure. That helps you in 2 ways. First, investors have to be able to understand how the business works so they can make intelligent decisions and minimize their risk. For some deals, it's a Securities and Exchange Commission (SEC) requirement that investors demonstrate a certain level of sophistication and risk tolerance in order to participate at all (we'll get into that later on). Second, potential business operators must be able to connect and communicate with brokers, sellers, and passive investors. If you don't know the lingo, you won't have any credibility. People won't give you the time of day if you sound like you don't know what you're talking about.

Let's start remedying that right now.

Throughout this book, you'll see terms we're introducing for the first time (or revisiting after a long time) set in **bold**. These terms will be important for you to learn and understand as you venture into the multifamily space.

The Basics of Apartment Syndication

As we covered in the Introduction, apartment syndication is a business model where a group of investors pool their money and resources to acquire a larger asset than they could afford on their own. For example, if you wanted to buy a $10 million property but you only had $100,000 to invest, how would you do it?

Well, if you needed to put 25% down on the purchase, that's $2.5 million. So you'd need 25 investors putting in $100,000 apiece. Then you could borrow the rest.

You wouldn't want to sign your own name and be personally on the hook for that $10 million, and the investors can't just Venmo $100,000 into your personal account. So you'd form a business entity—a Limited Liability Company (LLC) or Limited Partnership (LP)—and sell shares. The investors buy those shares. The new business entity then commits to the loan and purchases the property. These shares that are being sold are considered securities so you need to follow certain guidelines to make sure you are doing things the right way (more on this later).

LLCs are the most commonly used entity for syndications. However, if international investors will be involved in the deal, it's better to use an LP structure. In many countries, investors in an LLC are taxed domestically as well as in their home country since their home country does not recognize the LLC structure, but investors in an LP are not double-taxed. Our network has grown to include a number of international investors, so we always use the LP structure now to avoid the double taxation issue.

Now, an investor might actually have $2.5 million available—but they might not want to put it all in one place. Diversifying investments helps lower risk. This deep-pocket investor might buy 5 shares ($500,000) in each of 5 different offerings. If those offerings are in different cities, they'd have market diversification as well as asset diversification. However you slice the pie, you're still dividing the down payment on that property among however many people are participating.

So who are those people, what exactly are they investing in, and how do they get paid? Let's define some terms.

The Players

The operator is the individual or company that initiates and manages the business venture. They find the deal, draw up a business plan, create the new business entity, offer the shares, negotiate the purchase, find a lender, complete all the paperwork to acquire the property, and run the business until it's time to sell. The operator is sometimes called a **Sponsor** or a **General Partner**. We mostly use the term operator because it's the clearest—they operate the business operations. An operator invests sweat equity in the business and gets paid for their hard work.

Active investors are operators who also buy shares in multifamily deals and receive returns on that investment like any other limited partner or passive investor.

Passive investors put money into a multifamily deal for a return. They are shareholders in the business entity that owns the property. They receive regular payments out of the property's cash flow and (hopefully) a large payout when the property is finally sold. They don't have direct input into the day-to-day management of the business, but they should receive regular updates on how everything is going. Passive investors are sometimes called **Limited Partners**.

The Assets

In layman's terms, "multifamily" means any residential property with more than one dwelling unit. It could be a duplex or a small building with 4 or 5 apartments. In our industry—and for purposes of this book—the term **multifamily** indicates a larger building or complex with over five units. Anything smaller than that would be referred to simply as a "rental property." We focus our own business on properties with 100–350 units because they offer the best returns for our time and effort. We'll talk more in-depth about why larger assets are better investments in Chapter 2, but for now just keep in mind that a multifamily asset isn't a duplex—it's a community.

There are two sides to a multifamily asset: the physical and the financial. They are intertwined and affect each other, but there are important distinctions in the way we think about them and the way they're managed.

The **physical asset** consists of the property itself—buildings, amenities, and the land of an apartment complex. Just as with any type of real estate, the location and condition of the property affect its value. There are also abstract elements to the value of the physical asset. Those might include intangible features like the legal status of the title, the quality of the marketing, or the property's reputation with potential renters as a good place to live. All of these factors determine the amount of rent you can charge. The value of a commercial property is driven by its **net operating income (NOI)**. Net operating income is the revenue (mainly rent) minus expenses. An increase or decrease in the property's desirability to residents translates into an increase or decrease in rent, NOI, and ultimately value.

The physical asset could change value based on the operator's decisions—adding a swimming pool could make it more valuable, while neglecting maintenance could make it lose value. It could also change value due to outside factors, like an increase in demand for apartments because of a new major employer in town (or a decrease in demand if a big employer shuts down).

The **financial asset** is the business entity (the LLC or LP) that purchases the property, commits to the loan, and sells shares to investors. This entity is created solely for the purpose of buying a particular apartment complex, and will be dissolved when the property is eventually sold—that's why it's usually referred to as a **single-purpose entity (SPE)**.

The value of the financial asset is based largely on the value of the physical property, but there are many other factors that can affect its value separately. For example, the terms of the loan could make an investment more or less valuable as interest rates fluctuate. If the operator became financially unstable or untrustworthy in the way they run the business, that could lower the value of the investment regardless of the quality of the physical property.

A good multifamily investment is based on sound assets of both types: a valuable physical property and a reliable, well-managed financial asset.

The Returns

The SPE that owns the property produces profits. The operator and passive investors get paid out of that profit. Revenues from the property come in the form of rent and fees. Expenses get paid, like payroll, insurance, maintenance, etc. The excess goes back to the passive investors as cash flow.

Multifamily deals are usually set up for a specific period of time, with a margin of discretion so the operator can choose a good moment to sell based on market conditions. This planned term is called the **holding period**. Five years is a typical holding period in our business. A good operator will improve the property's value during the holding period so that it sells for more than the purchase price. That gain in value (after expenses) is also returned to the passive investors.

Ongoing returns are generally summarized as **cash-on-cash**. The amount of ongoing cash flow generated each year is averaged over the life of the investment and then expressed as a percentage of the initial investment. So, for your $100,000 share, how much income from operating profits will you expect to see each year? A 7% cash-on-cash return is a good benchmark, which would be $7,000 per year.

When the property is sold and the deal winds up, investors also receive a share of the proceeds. The sale proceeds averaged over the life of the deal, combined with annual cash-on-cash is usually expressed as **average annualized return (AAR)**.

Because multifamily is a real-estate business, the returns get special tax treatment that make this income even more valuable. We'll look at those aspects in more detail in Chapters 2 and 8.

Now that you have the ten-thousand-foot view of the business model, let's zoom in on the role of the operator and the foundational building blocks of running an apartment syndication business.

Becoming an Operator

We believe the best way to approach apartment syndication for the first time is as a passive investor with an established operator with a proven track record. You can reap the rewards from your first investment with the least effort, and you'll have an inside view on how the operator approaches every aspect of the business. However, not everyone has the initial capital to make that investment, and some people are just DIY'ers by temperament. So how can you get started as an operator?

Many new multifamily investors consider starting an apartment syndication business as a side hustle while they keep their regular day job. Indeed, there are a lot of coaches or gurus out there who will tell you it's a great part-time gig you can do nights and weekends. We hate to burst your bubble, but no! It just doesn't work that way.

We see it all the time—a brand-new operator comes in, full of energy and optimism. They put together one project and then you never hear from them again. Unfortunately, they didn't disappear because they struck gold and retired to a private island. They gave up because it's just too much work to try to maintain a day job and operate an apartment syndication business at the same time. We want to see people succeed, not burn out! That's why we emphasize that an apartment syndication business should be treated as a full-time business, not as a hobby.

Furthermore, operators have an obligation to their passive investors. Every one of our investors worked very hard for the money that they're entrusting to us. We owe it to them to work very hard to protect and increase the value of that investment. Would you sleep well at night knowing that you'd put a significant sum of money into somebody's side gig? We wouldn't. Becoming an operator is a full-time job if you're doing it right, and you have a duty to do it right.

Now that doesn't mean that if you still need your day job, you're stuck. There are several ways you can gain experience and learn the business of apartment syndication without trying to jump in as the main operator of a project right off the bat.

Paths to Success

The best way to learn the ins and outs of operating an apartment syndication business is to work part-time with an established operating group in a specific role. There are so many different skill sets required to successfully operate a multifamily project, a busy, growing group always needs help.

You can find opportunities to participate by networking with operators. You might be able to meet operators at local networking events. There are also national conferences you could attend to find these opportunities.

When you meet with a group, don't just ask them, "What do you need help with? I'll do anything you want me to do." That sounds friendly and flexible, but it isn't actually very useful from the operator's point of view. They don't need warm bodies. They need skills. You must understand where your skill set is, and what you can bring to the table. There are 4 main areas where you can enter the multifamily industry as a part-time venture and learn to become a successful operator: raising capital, underwriting, acquisition, and asset management. Let's look at the type of help and resources you could bring to each one.

RAISING CAPITAL

The apartment syndication business runs on relationships. If you already have a network of potential investors who might be interested in participating in a multifamily project, you could help a group raise capital through your network.In this scenario you bring equity to the table, which every operator needs. From a regulatory compliance perspective, that can't be your only role, so you would need to participate in other ways as well.

Here's why: bringing investors into a deal and getting paid for it is acting as a broker-dealer for compensation. Under SEC regulations, broker-dealers must be registered and licensed. If you're not, then you'd be subject to fines and civil penalties.

Raising capital is legal if you have an ownership stake in the General Partner (GP), or operating group, and contribute to another function as well. So you could invest your own money into the earnest money deposit. You could work on underwriting, asset management, or any of the other functions. The thing you need to avoid is getting paid based on the amount of money you bring in. That's "performance-based compensation," and it's a big no-no.

For example, you might agree to receive a 5% stake in the GP in exchange for raising $1 million and performing other duties. That's fine. But if you happen to raise $5 million in that same deal, you still only get 5%. If you get rewarded with a sliding scale based on the money raised, that's performance-based compensation, and you've run afoul of the SEC regulators. We aren't attorneys, so before you participate in a deal like this, we urge you to hire a good securities attorney and get everything in writing before you start raising a penny.

ACQUISITIONS

The process of touring and inspecting a property for acquisition involves a lot of legwork. A potential operator needs to tour the property and familiarize themselves with the local market and comparable properties in the area. Someone needs to be available and ready to meet brokers, property managers, investors, and competitors. They also need to understand what they're seeing and be able to give useful feedback to the operator. If you have the knowledge and experience, assisting with acquisition can be a great contribution to an operating group. We'll go in-depth on the process of finding and acquiring properties in Part 2.

UNDERWRITING

Underwriting is when you create your business plan for upgrading and operating the property. It requires skills in financial analysis, as well as knowledge about property management and construction and maintenance standards in the industry. You might have skills to bring on either side of that equation (or both). You'll learn more about the underwriting process in Chapter 4.

ASSET MANAGEMENT

Once an operator acquires a multifamily asset, they need to manage both the physical property and the financial operations of the asset as the owner. This requires a team of people with skills in property management, business management, communications, marketing, law, tax, accounting, and other general business functions. We'll unpack the physical and financial sides of asset management in Chapters 7 and 8.

Assemble Your Team

Now let's flip the scenario around. Let's say you've already gotten your feet wet by working with a successful operator. You've created enough cash flow from your part-time efforts to leave your day job. You're ready to go out on your own and organize your first project. Who do you need on your team to make sure you have all the skill sets—and the workload—covered?

First, we have the managing partners. The 2 of us (Dan and Danny) work full-time in our syndication business. As we mentioned in the Introduction, we have complementary skill sets with some overlap.

Between the 3 of us, we have experience in business development and management, financial analysis, property development, investor relations, and marketing.

At the beginning, we did everything ourselves. As we acquired more properties, we needed more help—and the revenue from those properties allowed us to afford the help. Now, with a dozen or more active projects, we maintain a staff of 30 people who work with us directly, on everything from communications to analysis to acquisitions.

We also use third-party contractors to outsource some specialties and hire on-site property management teams to handle the day-to-day details at the various properties. All together, we need about 75–100 people to keep this business running optimally. Let's break that down into our core staff or internal team, and our wider group of contractors, or the ancillary team.

YOUR INTERNAL TEAM

There are 4 core functions you need from your internal team: investor relations, acquisitions, asset management, and dispositions (selling the property when the holding period is over). We want to emphasize that at the beginning, we 3 were the internal team. When a potential newbie operator asks how much they should pay someone to help with acquisitions (or another core function), the answer is always, "Nothing!" For your first project, and maybe your first couple of projects, you should do it yourself.

Hands-on experience is vital for you to fully understand the details of how all the different roles need to work. That learning will help you hire more effectively later on. As you operate those early projects, you'll have several streams of income that you can reinvest into the business in order to grow your team. We made a commitment from the beginning that the asset management fees from our projects are always plowed back into the business itself. Then, as we close on more and more properties, we have more and more operating cash to work with, and we can hire the next team member. We're always looking ahead to identify the next 2 or 3 hires we'll need to develop our team to make sure we are protecting our investors' hard earned capital.

The issue of reinvesting profits brings up an important point for the passive investor. Just as you'd look for someone who's fully committed to their business instead of a part-timer, you should also look to invest with an operating group that's well-capitalized. Operators have several opportunities to profit from the business (and we'll go into more detail on those streams of income in the next section). If an operator is relying on the monthly cash flow from asset management fees in order to put food on the table, then they are in a financially precarious position. That revenue should be put to work managing the asset—*your* asset. An operator that's stretched too thin won't be able to monitor the performance of that property or cope with risks and problems in the business. Look for a robust operation with room to grow.

When you hire, make sure you're setting the right priorities for each position. Some team members need experience in the real estate industry. Others need to be specialists in their discipline and industry experience isn't as important. For example, when we chose our director of marketing and public relations, her most important qualification was excellence in those skills. She didn't necessarily need a background in apartment syndication, per se. The same is true for our video producer and editor. For hiring in investor relations, we look for a background in sales. People with these specialized skills can learn about real estate, but real estate experience wouldn't make them a talented designer or salesperson.

On the other hand, it's more important for members of your acquisition and disposition teams to have a real-estate background. That's why your own hands-on experience will be so helpful in hiring—you'll understand the skills and talents necessary for each role and have a good sense of which candidates are likely to be the most valuable.

At this point in our business growth, we have all our potential hires take an assessment before their initial interview to gauge their cognitive ability, motivation, and personality. This screening tool reveals how well-matched they are for the position and for our team. We use (and recommend) the Wonderlic test, which is also used by the NFL and major companies like DuPont. Your internal team is the backbone of your business. It pays to make sure you're hiring well.

You may not need to hire all your team members full-time. Some of these roles are exactly the sort of opportunities that future operators are seeking as a part-time introduction to the business. Others might be a great fit for knowledgable people who like the industry but don't want to take the risk of operating on their own. Hiring part-time help is a great way to ramp up your internal operations gradually. However, when you hire part-time work, you usually get what you pay for. Most part-time people are using it as a stopgap while they look for full-time work or plan to be an operator themselves one day. Keep this in mind when hiring part-time workers.

You may even start out by filling some of these niches with contractors as part of your ancillary team. Let's look at how your ancillary team can support you starting out and on an ongoing basis.

YOUR ANCILLARY TEAM

Building an ancillary team is essential from the outset. You should be able to cover your core business functions on your own, but your ancillary team will support you with specialized knowledge that you'll have to outsource. These team members include your real estate attorney, your transactional attorney, your securities attorney, your CPA and tax consultant, your property management company, your insurance broker, and other professional service roles. Creative or support roles like graphic design, photography, copywriting, or bookkeeping could start out as ancillary contractors, too. We started out using freelance virtual assistants to develop our pitch decks and investor materials, and that's a great, affordable way to bootstrap into growing your team.

Some real estate gurus will advise you to have every member of your ancillary team in place ahead of time. It's smart to network and have a general idea of who you could call on to fill some of these roles, but we don't find it a good use of your time to try to nail everything down too far in the future. It's better to start working on a deal and finding passive investors first, even if you don't have your whole team lined up.

After all, professionals don't want to spend their time on tire-kickers. A lot of people want free advice for vague business ideas and nobody takes them seriously. If you show up with a deal underway and ask for advice or referrals on a real project, they will take you seriously. If the first person you ask isn't able or available to help, ask them for a recommendation. By following those referrals, you'll be able to move quickly and find the right person to help you with your first deal. You'll also build your network of relationships, which is incredibly valuable in this business.

One of the most important characteristics to look for in your ancillary team (besides knowledge in their field) is responsiveness. If you're working on a **purchase and sale agreement (PSA)** with your real estate attorney, and it takes them two or three days to respond to every change, you could lose the deal. If you won a deal by promising to expedite closing, you will need to get your due diligence done in 30 days or less. If your CPA works at a slow pace and can't provide your tax documents on time, all your investors might have to file extensions on their own tax returns. They won't be happy. Delays like that create headaches and can even cause you to lose investors. Your ancillary team needs to be on the ball and have the capacity to turn around big projects on short notice, especially with closings.

The quality of your ancillary team can make or break your reputation with the parties you negotiate with or hurt your relationships with your investors, which hurts your business in the long term. Choose wisely.

How Operators Get Paid

Operators earn fees for the work they do organizing and managing the apartment syndication business. Some of them are one-time fees paid at particular milestones of the deal. Others are ongoing fees over the life of the project. The third type are equity splits based on the performance of the asset. Many of these fees are paid by the SPE that owns the physical asset before the profits are distributed to the passive investors. So essentially, they are paid by the passive investors to the operator.

The operator has a certain amount of discretion as to which fees to charge and the rates for each fee. When you're planning your own apartment syndication business, you have to bear in mind that the more fees you charge, the harder it will be for you to find a deal that passes underwriting. The higher your fees, the lower the passive investors' returns will be. If you overfee yourself, you'll have a very hard time attracting investors, because investors want to see healthy returns on their money and will choose a different project.

Some operators claim they don't charge fees at all, but when you look closely at the deal structure, they are just taking their profits out of a different part of the revenue stream. Deals like that often have an even lower return for the investors because those fees aren't actually gone. They're just hidden. We don't recommend doing business that way.

Beyond fees, operators also earn shares of the asset's revenue once it meets certain benchmarks, and shares of the profit when the property sells. Those are referred to as **equity splits**. We'll look at equity splits in detail in Chapter 5 when we discuss deal structuring.

Let's look at some of the most common operator fees and then some that are less commonly seen.

COMMON OPERATOR FEES

The **acquisition fee** is very straightforward. These are fees paid to the operator for putting the deal together and acquiring the asset.

Acquisition fees are calculated as a percentage of the purchase price, or as a percentage of the **total transaction amount**. Typical acquisition fees would range from 2% to 5%, depending on the size of the deal. The higher the purchase price of an asset, the lower the percentage, while a smaller purchase price would carry fees at the higher end of the range. It's the same amount of work for an operator to put together a $5 million deal as a $50 million deal, so the fee should stay in proportion.

Total transaction amount includes the purchase price, closing costs, capital expenditures, and any additional money raised from the investors for an operating reserve.

Capital expenditure (CapEx) is the amount of money needed to improve the physical property to achieve your business plan. For example, if you needed to renovate the units, replace the roof, paint the buildings' exteriors, or resurface the parking lot, those would all be considered part of your CapEx budget.

An **operating reserve** is a financial cushion that many operators include in their capital raising so the new entity has cash on hand to pay for general operating expenses until revenue starts coming in, and in case of emergencies.

The **asset management fee** is paid monthly to the operator for their ongoing services in managing the business. (This is the revenue stream we consistently reinvest in growing our business and hiring more team members). Asset management fees can be as high as 5% of gross monthly income from the property but typically are between 1% and 3%. Another common way to calculate this fee is to base it on a percentage of the total equity in the deal, calculated on an annual basis. For example, if $12 million was raised to acquire an asset, then a 1% fee would allow for $120,000 per year to be paid to manage the asset ($12,000,000 × 1% = $120,000). This annual amount would still be paid out in installments of $10,000 per month.

A principle we use in our business is that we treat our asset management fees as performance-based. As long as the property is generating cash flow and we are making distributions to our investors, we take our asset management fees. However, if something goes wrong and we can't make that distribution, we don't get paid either. We just don't feel that it's right for us to siphon cash from the property if it's not performing well. That doesn't mean we'll never get paid. For example, we'll still receive those fees when the property sells (assuming we sell it at sufficient profit). We just believe that our obligation is to protect the investors, and so we don't collect a fee for managing the asset if the investors aren't getting paid.

Property management fees are, as the name suggests, paid for property management—the day-to-day functions of marketing, leasing, and maintaining the physical property. Many operators work with third-party property managers, as we do. In that case the property management fees go directly to the third party. Some operator groups are vertically integrated and maintain their own property management division. In that case, they would collect this fee themselves. These fees can vary widely, from 2.5% all the way up to 10% or 12%.

Property management fees tend to be inversely proportional to the size of the property. If you're buying an asset with less than a hundred units, you may have a harder time finding a property management company to work with and may have to pay fees on the higher end.

We strongly recommend that new operators outsource their property management. When you're starting a new apartment syndication business, it's a bad idea to start a second business at the same time. Furthermore, lenders don't like it. Lenders are the largest single investor in your project, and they vet every part of the deal, including the track record of the management company. If they have no confidence that you can manage the asset, you'll have a hard time finding a loan. As you build up your portfolio, you could start a vertically-integrated property management company for your own assets. When you're starting out, it's best to use an experienced third party.

The **disposition fee** is paid when you sell the asset. After you perform your business plan, you've increased the profitability of the community and the value of the asset, then you sell the asset and receive the disposition fee. This fee is based on the final sale price and typically ranges from 1% to 3%.

In the same way that we tie the asset management fee to the asset's performance, our group also makes the disposition fee performance-based: we set a minimum return threshold, and if we meet or exceed that threshold, the fee is activated.

For example, if we project a 15% annualized return for our investors, and we deliver it (or more), our disposition fee kicks in. Some groups work differently—they take their disposition fee out of the sale whether the investors make their projected return or not. The difference is that we are investors in every one of our projects, and we always want to structure our deals as if we were putting up all the money ourselves. We protect our investors as much as possible, and we just wouldn't feel right taking money off an asset that didn't meet the investors' objectives.

An **annualized return** shows the annual rate of return averaged over a period of time.

We'll go into more depth about performance-based deal structures, waterfalls, and equity splits in Chapter 5.

A **capital event fee** (sometimes called a refinancing fee) is paid to the operator when you refinance an asset or take on a supplemental loan. With some deals, you may have a permanent loan that can't be refinanced due to prepayment penalties or other obstacles. However, it might be advantageous to get a supplemental loan on the property. For example, if you've held an asset for a couple of years and substantially increased its value, you might want to pull some equity out of the property and return it to the investors. Refinancing can allow you to do that.

A capital event fee reflects the effort and negotiation involved in arranging that refinance or supplemental loan, and the value to the investors of having that capital returned to them early. Typical capital event fees range from 1% to 3% of the capital that was pulled out of the property and are taken from the proceeds of the loan or refinance. The amount may be based on the amount of the loan or on the overall new value of the property. Our group doesn't charge capital event fees, but they are one of the more common fees in the industry.

The **loan guarantor fee** is paid to the person who signs on the loan in order to guarantee repayment. Lenders require the guarantor to be an individual with sufficient net worth and liquidity to make the loan good in case of default by the operator. This fee may be calculated on the loan amount, on the purchase price, or on the total transaction amount, depending on the deal structure. It usually ranges between 1% and 3%.

LESS COMMON OPERATOR FEES

There are a number of other possible fees that an operator can charge. Some of them may not apply to every deal. Others are discretionary.

Construction management fees may be charged when a property needs significant renovation after acquisition. They usually range from 5% to 10% of the renovation budget. Whether this fee is paid to the operator or the property management company depends on whether the property manager is overseeing the renovation or the operator is managing it in-house.

Our group doesn't charge construction management fees, and our property managers don't either. We feel that it creates a conflict of interest. After all, if we are making money on the renovations, that's an incentive to continue renovating beyond the point that it's in the investors' best interest. We never want to be in a position where we have to choose between the investors making money and the operating group making money. Our interests should be aligned.

A **brokerage fee** is one of the least common operator fees. It's more commonly paid to a broker who isn't directly involved in a deal but introduces the parties to each other. You might think of it as a finder's fee. It's usually calculated as 1% to 3% of the purchase price.

If an operator who is already receiving an acquisition fee wants to also receive a brokerage fee on the same deal, that's a big red flag that passive investors should pay attention to. They're asking to be paid twice for the same job, which indicates they're probably charging too many fees overall.

For new operators, we also want to warn you against a practice you may see in some multifamily mentoring groups. There are groups that will advise you not to charge any fees but expect you to pay a brokerage fee in order to work with them. So they get paid, but you don't. We think that's unethical and should be avoided at all costs.

There are many different revenue streams available for operators, enough to grow your business and see healthy returns for your hard work. The truly priceless asset in this business is your passive investors' confidence. However you set up your fee structure, make sure that you're putting your investors' best interests first. That relationship and reputation will reap long-term rewards long after an individual deal is over.

Language Immersion

We've thrown a lot of concepts and terms at you in this chapter, and we'll continue to introduce more terminology throughout the book. It's important that you don't just know these terms on paper. You need to internalize them and understand them in real-world situations. The best way to do that is just like learning any foreign language: immersion. You need to live within the culture and absorb it from every side. A great place to start is to join Facebook groups dedicated to multifamily investing so you can participate in discussions on these topics every day. But you need to go deeper.

You can request to join our private Facebook group at https://www.facebook.com/groups/multifamilyinvestornation.

We teach new operators to sharpen their skills through practice—but not in the market where you actually plan to invest. As we mentioned earlier, your business depends on cultivating relationships with brokers, sellers, and other investors, so you don't want to blow your credibility while you're still learning. If you start talking with a broker in your own market and you make an embarrassing blunder, you could blow your chances of making a deal through that broker later on because first impressions matter. They might advise a seller that you didn't seem competent. Remember, your reputation is one of your biggest assets and it instills confidence in your partners and your business network.

Instead, find a market that's at least two states away geographically from your target market. Identify some brokers there and call them up. Talk to them and ask questions. Take them to lunch, tour properties, talk about underwriting some of the deals they're handling, and participate in the business culture.

Be prepared to make mistakes—it's inevitable. You'll sound foolish sometimes. If they realize that you don't really know what cash-on-cash means, or that you don't understand some of the technical underwriting terms we'll cover later on, that's okay! You're not going to be working with them anyway.

Hopefully, you're beginning to understand why we talk about operating an apartment syndication business as a full-time job. It's a great business to be in, but there are a lot of moving parts involved in doing it right, and doing it profitably.

Now that we've sketched out the basic overview, let's start to unpack why large apartment complexes are such a good investment and the benefits they bring to active and passive investors.

Chapter 2

Why Invest in Large Apartments?

Danny Randazzo

Rental properties are a pain in the butt! Everybody knows that, right? Your disgruntled cousin knows. Your wacky aunt tells you every Thanksgiving, "Never own a rental property. Do you want to get calls at three o'clock in the morning to go clean out someone's toilet? Do you want to spend your weekends worrying about how to replace a broken fridge? It's a miserable life."

Not so fast.

I agree with Mr. or Ms. Opinionated that owning a single-family rental can be an awful lot of work—sometimes more work than it's worth. Your margins between revenue and expenses are pretty tight, and you'll probably need to do a lot of the hands-on work yourself. Your income isn't predictable because it depends on 1 tenant paying their rent on time. If they move out, your property isn't generating any income until you get a new tenant in. If a major system like the water heater or sewer line goes out, it could wipe out the income from a whole quarter—or maybe a whole year.

Investing in large apartment communities is entirely different. You aren't the one getting those 3 a.m. phone calls. You won't lose your whole revenue stream when a tenant moves out or some equipment breaks. You can project your returns and expect them to stay quite stable. And you don't have to stick your hand in anybody's toilet.

In this chapter we'll look at the benefits of investing in institutional, quality apartment complexes. These fall into three main areas: the security and stability of the investment, tax advantages, and the ability to invest in a hands-off, hassle-free structure.

Security

Warren Buffet's number one rule of investing is "Don't lose money." Owning large apartments is a lower risk investment compared to alternative investment options. It's a great place to store your hard earned capital and protect it. That's due to a number of factors, some of which apply to real estate in general, and some of which are specific to large apartment communities: high demand, low volatility, recession resistance, and forced appreciation.

Demand

The great thing about the multifamily business is that you're selling a necessity. Some people want to start businesses doing things they personally enjoy, like running a restaurant or an arts-and-crafts store. As an investor or entrepreneur, the downside to those business models is their risk and volatility. Nobody really *needs* those fancy appetizers or silk flowers, so you're constantly trying to generate demand, and you're very sensitive to changes in the economy.

For my money, I want to invest in a business with constant demand. With multifamily real estate, we provide people with housing (in our niche, very nice housing). In fact, when the economy weakens, demand for rental apartments usually goes up because people don't want to tie up their money in purchasing a new home.

As the population of the United States (and the world) increases, we're seeing that most people choose to rent an apartment over buying their own house. The demand for apartments is ever-present and strengthening. Roughly 50% of the population in the United States choose to rent apartments. This allows apartment communities to maintain solid occupancy. Occupancy means steady revenue and the strong possibility to have the property increase in value over time.

Low Volatility

When we talk about stability and security, these are great advantages that real estate has over investing in stocks and bonds or other instruments. The price of a stock is so volatile because both rational and irrational reasons cause it to fluctuate. If you own a pharmaceutical stock and the company's new drug fails FDA approval, the price could bottom out. But the same thing can happen due to rumors, or politics, or the behavior of big Wall Street investors.

When you own real estate in the right market with the right economic indicators, the value of your investment remains much more stable. Backed by a real, physical asset with demonstrable performance, it's less dependent on outside factors. Typically, over 5 or 10 years, your property will be at least as valuable as the day you bought it, if not more. You also have the ability to control the care and improvement of the asset. You can't do anything to influence the value of a stock, but you can make real changes to an apartment community that pay off in real gains.

Wall Street doesn't really want you to know about apartment investing. They want to keep your money in the market, actively trading stocks and bonds, or paying them fees to do it for you. They're the middleman, and they don't care whether you win or lose. They get paid either way. Wall Street and big banks don't educate investors about the power of investing in real estate, especially in apartment communities, because it's not in their best interest. It's vital that you understand all the investment strategies that are available to you, so you can make the best decisions to reach your personal and family goals.

Recession Resistance

As an asset class, apartment communities have typically performed better than alternative investments during market cycles. That includes stocks and bonds, single-family properties, and commercial and retail real estate. Furthermore, the value of real estate moves much slower in a market cycle than stocks and bonds do. A typical market downturn lasts twelve to eighteen months before the economy recovers. A long cycle can have long-term impacts on your investment capital if you are forced to liquidate assets while prices are still low. Because multifamily properties generate monthly cash flow, you have the ability to time the market cycle and sell at a more advantageous season.

As the owner of an apartment community, you're in the enviable position of never really being forced to sell an asset. When there are ups and downs in the market cycle, you can hold that asset and continue receiving income every month. When the economy recovers, you've weathered the storm. So owning large apartment communities can be a recession-resistant investment approach if executed properly.

If you're an active operator, you'll need to take steps to ensure that you can control your investment horizon. As a passive investor, you want to make sure you're placing your money with an experienced operator who understands how to navigate the 12 to 18 month economic cycles that happen from time to time. Either way, large apartment communities are a great way to protect your capital in challenging times.

Forced Appreciation

One important difference between investing in single-family rental properties and large apartment communities is the way that they're valued. The price of an ordinary house greatly depends on the prices of comparable houses in the neighborhood, your "comps." If the house on the corner is smaller than yours and sold for $200,000, and the house down the street is bigger and sold for $300,000, and your house is right in the middle, then it should sell for $250,000. You can spruce up the curb appeal, but you have no control over the major factors that influence the value of your property.

Large apartment communities are valued based on the annual income they generate. The more income a property brings in, the more valuable it is. This is something you can control. As you learned in Chapter 1, NOI is the revenue from the building minus expenses. As an active operator, you have the ability to force-appreciate the value of the asset by increasing the NOI.

You can achieve increases in net income many different ways. You can improve the property, making it more attractive to renters, which allows you to charge more rent. You can make strategic additions that generate revenue, like adding laundry equipment or providing internet service for a fee. You could make the operations more efficient and reduce expenses, which also increases the net income. All these changes force the value of the property up.

For the passive investor, it's essential that you choose an operator who understands how to protect and increase the value of your asset over time.

Stabilized Operations

Large apartment communities have size and scale that allow you to predict your income and expenses on a normalized basis. For example, in a single-family rental, if your one resident leaves, then your property immediately goes from 100% occupied to 0% occupied. Your income, therefore, immediately drops to zero as well. By contrast, if you own a 100-unit community, all 100 units won't go vacant at the same time. If one resident leaves, your occupancy drops by 1%, which isn't a material impact on the business. Those sudden ups and downs are smoothed out.

In industry terms, a **stable asset** is one that has at least 90% physical occupancy for a minimum of 3 months, and a property that doesn't meet those criteria is referred to as **nonstable** or **nonperforming** (unless it is brand-new and still filling up. The term for that phase is **prestabilized**). **Physical occupancy** refers to how many units are leased to a resident. Now, **economic occupancy** is a different matter—that refers to how many physically occupied units are paying rent. If you had a hundred units in your complex, leased at $1,000 per month rent, you should be collecting $100,000 per month. If some of those residents are behind on their rent, you might only collect $70,000. In that case, you'd be at 100% physical occupancy but only 70% economic occupancy. We'll talk more about the implications of physical and economic occupancy in Chapter 6.

The larger volume of residents on your property generates a larger volume of cash flow. This allows you to easily absorb unanticipated expenses. A single-family rental might cash flow a few hundred dollars a month, so major expenses can create major crises. A large community with 100 to 300 units generates 100 to 300 times more cash each month. That level of revenue can cover a new water heater or a roof repair without any significant impact on the business's overall performance.

Furthermore, the scale of a multifamily asset allows—really, it requires—you to use professional property management services. Compared to a single-family rental, investing in a large community gives you a much better return on your time. Back in Chapter 1, we talked about the fact that becoming an operator is a full-time business, and that's certainly true. Here we're looking at the nature of the work you're doing and how you're compensated for it.

With smaller properties, you'll be faced with much more of the hands-on labor of property management (like those 3 a.m. calls about the toilet). Large apartment communities are overseen by professional management companies. A professional property management team has the manpower and efficiency to handle that aspect of the on-site work in a way you, as the investor, never could. When you stick with multifamily assets, you can be a real estate investor without the hassle of becoming a landlord. While you're sleeping, your money is still working.

All these factors—consistent demand, consistent value, strong performance in market cycles, the ability to control appreciation, and stabilized operations—make large apartment communities a stable and secure investment. Let's look at the tax advantages that make it even better.

Tax Benefits of Multifamily Investing

Real estate investing brings one of the biggest tax benefits in the world: depreciation on your assets. The long-term goal of investing is to increase your capital. As soon as you realize those capital gains, they become taxable. Every year you own real estate, you can claim depreciable losses that offset those gains and reduce your tax liability.

How much difference does it really make? Typically, if you had an apartment investment that generated 8% to 9% annual cash flow, you'd need to see 13% to 15% gain per year from an investment in stocks or bonds to have a comparable after-tax return.

To compare apples to apples, let's say you had a stock investment that produced a 10% annual dividend, and a real estate investment that produced a 10% cash-on-cash return. Your gain on the real estate would be covered by depreciable losses, so that you'd keep the whole 10% return. On the other hand, your stock dividend would be taxed, yielding a net return of 7% to 8%.

We'll go into detail on tax strategies for passive and active investors (and how they differ) in Chapter 10. Owning large apartment communities is a great step toward reducing your taxable income and providing advantages that alternative investments simply can't match. When you're evaluating investment opportunities and checking the boxes for pros and cons, the tax advantages of apartment communities are a substantial box in the "pro" column.

Beyond all these advantages of time, money, and tax savings, I believe one of the biggest benefits of multifamily investing is that you can reap so many of the rewards while staying completely hands-off from the grunt work of running the business. So let's really dig into the benefits of passive investing in large apartments.

Passive Investing for the Win

I want to share a story with you about one of our real-life investors. I'll call her Susie, for privacy's sake. Susie tragically lost her husband when they were in their mid-50s. Her husband had always handled the family finances, and she felt overwhelmed. She was left with a teenager to raise by herself, and her income as a teacher just wasn't enough to support them. Susie was always taught to make sure she never spent more money than she made in a month. Thankfully, Susie and her husband set up life insurance, so she at least received a life insurance benefit when he died. So even while she was still grieving, she set that insurance money aside for her child's future and took on a second job driving Uber at night to make ends meet.

When she learned about passive investing in large apartment communities, it opened up new possibilities for her family. She placed some of that insurance money into a multifamily project, knowing that it was a secure investment to protect that nest egg. It also generated a monthly income that allowed her to quit Uber and spend more time with her child, which they both needed so badly.

That direct deposit into her bank account every month helped her to be confident in her new role as the head of the family finances. It freed up her time and gave her peace of mind that she had enough income each month to pay the bills. Taking the plunge to invest in something new or different can be scary—it was for Susie—but it was the best option for her to put that capital to work.

Now, because Susie joined us as a passive investor, she doesn't need to do any work in the business on a regular basis. Her money does the work for her. She just receives an automatic direct deposit every month.

Susie did her work up front by learning to understand multifamily assets as an investment vehicle, rather than a business she wanted to operate (after all, her goal was to work less and spend more time with her family). If she wants to stay engaged, she can read her monthly email updates about the property's performance, but that's the extent of her responsibility going forward.

Susie's story illustrates the real power of multifamily investing to shape your future. Susie isn't some high-net-worth professional investor. She's an ordinary working mom who was able to place a modest amount of capital in a business that changed her family's lifestyle for the better.

Where to Begin

The first requirement to begin investing in large apartments—like any investment—is that you need some money to invest. Even if you plan to work as an active operator, you'll probably need to use some money of your own. It's possible to start on a shoestring budget and just invest sweat equity, but you'll have a hard time convincing sophisticated investors to trust you with their money if you don't have any skin in the game. It's much easier to get started as an active investor if you have funds set aside to start that business and invest so others will feel confident enough to invest alongside you.

For the passive investor, you can typically get started for about $25,000 on the low end (but the minimum investment will vary from deal to deal based on the operator). There are some online opportunities where you can get started with a minimum of a few hundred dollars, but it's all relative to your personal goals and what you want to achieve.

You don't need to invest a ton of money your first time out. I do recommend you have some capital to get started. It makes the process easier, and you can achieve your goals in a faster timeline.

WHO CAN INVEST?

Multifamily investing is regulated by the SEC. In order to protect the public, the SEC requires potential investors to meet certain requirements before they can invest. These criteria sort eligible investors into two groups: accredited and non-accredited (non-accredited investors are sometimes called "sophisticated" investors). Multifamily projects may be open to only accredited investors, or they may be open to both types, depending on the way the deal is structured.

The two main ways to qualify as an **accredited investor** are based on your net worth or your income:

- You must have at least $1 million of net worth that does not include your primary residence, or

- You must have an annual income of at least $200,000 per year if you're single or $300,000 per year if you're married. You must have had that income for at least two years and have a reasonable expectation that it will continue.

Now, there is no formal process or official documentation to be qualified as an accredited investor. I've actually seen some sleazy CPAs try to charge their clients $5,000 to be qualified. That's hogwash!

All you need is a letter from your attorney, financial advisor, or CPA confirming that you meet the criteria. That's it. If you were previously verified, as long as the letter is dated within the last ninety days, we can still accept it. Once we accept a verification, our previous investors don't have to keep getting verified for each deal. The verification is good for five years.

If you don't have a professional who is familiar with your finances, or they don't want to issue the letter, there are third-party companies that can review your documentation and issue a confirmation letter for between $60 and $80. We currently work with the third-party service Parallel Markets, Inc. When we set this up for our investors, we pay the fee. This should not be a hoop you have to jump through.

Non-accredited, or **sophisticated investors** might not meet the income or net worth requirements, but they have prior experience in business or finance and experience investing outside the stock market. Sophisticated investors must also have an existing relationship with the operator of a project. This protects people who don't really understand what they're doing from being lured into a bum deal by fast-talking strangers. You don't need a third party to confirm your status as a non-accredited investor. You would just sign a document attesting to your own experience and prior relationship.

Your Self-Directed Future

One of the most important reasons to invest in large apartment communities is that you can take control of your financial freedom. When it comes to investing your personal resources in multifamily communities, there are many different avenues to get started. You may have capital available through your personal business or LLC. You could use funds in a retirement account. You might even have cash in your checking or savings account that's just sitting at a miniscule interest rate, losing value all the time to inflation.

Perhaps you have money sitting stagnant in a 401k account from an old employer. These types of managed accounts usually have a very limited slate of mutual funds to choose from and pretty disappointing results. Instead, you could roll that money into a self-directed IRA or 401k with a custodian and place your funds in a multifamily project. You can take charge of your options and your results, and choose an investment with the size and scale to deliver on your personal investment goals.

CUSTODIAL RETIREMENT ACCOUNTS

About 20% to 25% of our investors invest through some sort of self-directed retirement vehicle. The thing is, you have to make sure your account is set up the right way. If you call up Charles Schwab or Fidelity or another brokerage that you may have a retirement account with, and ask to self-direct the account, they'll say "Sure!" The problem is, they'll only allow you to self-direct it within the products that they sell. As we mentioned earlier, Wall Street isn't interested in selling apartment syndications or letting you control your own money. In order to truly self-direct your retirement funds, you'll have to move to a self-directed custodian. There are a number of companies that can act as custodians of your self-directed IRA.

A few custodial companies are Advanta IRA, Equity Trust Company, IRA Financial, The Entrust Group, and Alto IRA. Be sure to do your own research and check with a few different custodians to ensure they meet your needs.

The process is quite straightforward. You simply request a new account from the custodial company, and they'll send you the forms you need to complete. You'd submit those forms to your current brokerage or retirement account manager, and the account would be rolled over into your self-directed account with the custodial company you select.

Let's say you move $300,000 in that newly created self-directed account, and you want to invest passively in multifamily businesses. You could allocate different amounts to different projects: $50,000 to one, $75,000 to another, $125,000 to a third. So you're diversifying your self-directed account into multiple assets, and whenever there are cash flows off of those properties, your self-directed account will automatically get the cash flow distributions.

One of the major limitations with ordinary retirement accounts is that you are limited to stocks or a small number of exchanged-traded funds (ETFs) and mutual funds. This self-directed structure is a great way to put your retirement funds to work outside the stock market, avoid its volatility, and control your hard-earned money!

The main caveat you should be aware of is that you can't use a self-directed retirement account to invest in a deal that you control as the main operator or general partner. That means for operators and active investors, you would have to become a passive investor in another group's asset. We actually have a network among other well-known operators that invest their custodial funds in our properties, and we invest in theirs. When you find other groups that you know, like, and trust, you can form these mutual connections, and it's really cool to see how everyone can win together.

Making the Connections

No matter where your funds are sitting now, putting them to work in multifamily assets can give you more control over your future prosperity. There's a lot more to know about passive investing, including how to set up a passive investing strategy, what you need to know about underwriting a deal, how to choose an operator to invest with, and advanced strategies for legacy wealth building. We'll focus on passive investing in-depth in Part 4. For now, let's look at how new operators can build relationships with investors and what investors should expect when an operator is committed to cultivating a great long-term relationship.

Chapter 3

Developing Your Investor Relations Process

Dan Handford

In this apartment syndication business, you're going to be constantly looking for two things: new deals and new passive investors. If you find the perfect deal and have nobody ready to invest, you can't take advantage of the opportunity. Or worse, you will lose the deal because you couldn't perform, which will tarnish your reputation with brokers, sellers, and passive investors. Once you find qualified, eager investors, you won't actually be able to work with them until you have a deal ready for them to invest their capital into. It's a two-edged sword. The old chicken-and-egg scenario.

Since 2018, our group at PassiveInvesting.com has raised over half a billion dollars from private, high-net-worth investors (HNWI) investors (see Figure X for a breakdown of our track record on raising capital year-over-year). This capital was not from institutional investors like real estate investment trusts (REITs), hedge funds, family offices, banks, or other organizations that have tons of money to invest. This capital was raised from everyday real estate investors that we've cultivated relationships with. The key words here are "cultivated relationships": this is of the utmost importance to your investor relations process. Cultivating relationships should be the cornerstone of the entire process. Investors want to be treated like real people—your friends, not just numbers.

We were able to raise this extraordinary amount of capital from ordinary people because we focus on building relationships with them. We base everything we do on authenticity, transparency, and accountability in those relationships. Asking someone to place their hard-earned money, or their childrens' inheritance, into an asset you're managing is a huge responsibility. You have to earn their trust, and you have to be worthy of that trust. When you keep that relationship strong, it will continue to create new relationships over time.

Your relationships with your investors are so important, I'm actually devoting 2 chapters to it. In this chapter, I'll introduce you to the natural cycle that builds trust and grows your investor network. I'll also discuss the technical and legal reasons why you need to document your investor relations process, as well as the pros and cons of institutional versus private equity.

In the next chapter, I'll teach you the exact system we use to cultivate our massive investor network and secure hundreds of millions in private capital. If you're an aspiring operator, you can—and should—start using this system on a small scale because it will grow with you. For the passive investor, I'm happy for you to see the way the system works, too. There are no tricks. There's nothing going on behind-the-scenes that you shouldn't see. The system exists to make sure you are fully informed and dialed in to what's going on with your investment at all times.

Relationship Matters

Now, from the perspective of the operator, to find investors and turn them into repeat investors, you need to understand the natural cycle a new passive investor goes through. We call it our Investor Triad. If you're doing it right, you'll have investors stay with you for many years, investing in multiple deals. Better yet, they'll refer other investors to you, who will continue to invest with you for many years as well. In order to understand our investor relations process, you have to understand the mindset of an investor.

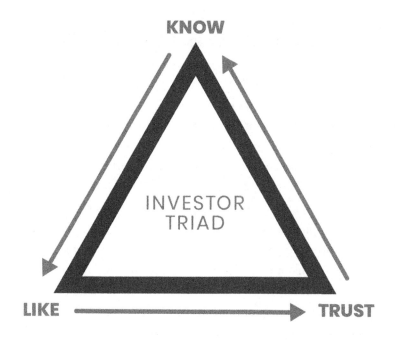

The Investor Triad sums it up: Know, Like, and Trust. You've probably heard that combination before. Think about it for a minute before you continue reading: which one do you think is most important?

Most people I ask will say "Trust." That's completely understandable because an investor isn't going to work with you if they don't trust you. Some people will say "Like" because nobody is going to listen to you long enough to trust you if they don't already like you.

However, both options are incorrect. Neither Like nor Trust are the most important. The most important element in the Investor Triad is "*Know.*"

If passive investors don't know who you are, then they'll never have an opportunity to formulate an opinion as to whether or not they like or trust you. How can they like or trust you until they know you even exist?

Now, as soon as someone gets to know you, they form an opinion of you, usually within a matter of seconds. Research has shown that it only takes about 30 seconds for someone to decide whether they like you or not. So they'll decide whether they like you or not pretty quickly. The more investors who get to know that you even exist, the more people will pick a side.

Of course, you'll always encounter some investors who don't like you. You can't worry about them. You have to just stay true to yourself and let people know who you really are. Never try to "fake it until you make it" in this business. Investors are savvy and will read right past your facade. I have seen it before in this industry, and those groups go under really quickly as investors figure out what's going on.

When people like you, they'll start to connect with you and open up to the opportunity for ongoing communication. That lets them see how you think and how you operate, so they can make the bigger decision of whether they trust you with their hard-earned capital.

You'll see in the diagram that there are arrows from Know to Like, and from Like to Trust. There's also an arrow from Trust back to Know. You might be thinking, "They already know me. How does this connect back to knowing me again?" That's where referrals come in. You know you have completed the process successfully when your existing investors are so happy that they begin referring their own family, friends, and colleagues to you.

When an investor likes and trusts you enough to invest their money with you, you prove that trust was warranted by managing the relationship well and delivering the returns they expected. Then they'll start reaching out to family, friends, and colleagues to refer them to you. Now you know more people, and as a bonus, they're coming into the relationship with good expectations because of that personal introduction. It's immediate credibility. The nice thing is that referred investors don't need a ton of time to hang around in the Like phase. They're ready to trust you right away because of the power of the referral.

Often, we'll release a deal to our investors, and as soon as they get the email announcement, they'll start referring other passive investors to us by forwarding the email to their network. These new contacts are already prepared to invest in the deal because they trust the person that sent them. They say things like, "Oh, I've known her for 15 years. She's put her own money into this and she wouldn't invest if it weren't legit."

They did their due diligence on their relationship with the person who referred them, so they don't feel a need to start over doing due diligence on you. This cycle is the pinnacle of a healthy investor relations process. Of course, even with eager referrals, we still have our process in place. We don't skip steps. They're investing with us, and we invest in them with ongoing communication and reliability. That's what makes a long-term investor relationship work.

Relationship Requirements

These investor relationships also matter in raising capital for legal reasons. As Danny mentioned in Chapter 2, there are regulatory requirements for investors in these types of multifamily investments. You have your accredited, high-net-worth investors, and you have your non-accredited, sophisticated investors. As an operator, whether you bring both types of investors into a deal or accredited investors only, depends on the deal structure you choose.

There are two different regulatory structures for multifamily syndication projects. These are governed by the SEC in Regulation D, Rule 506. These types of deals typically fall under either Rule 506(b) or Rule 506(c). Less commonly, you will see offerings under Regulation A+, but we don't use those structures in every deal.

You can find a summary of these regulatory structures in our Apartment Syndication Toolkit at PassiveInvesting.com/Toolkit.

Let's break down the two main offering types and also touch on the Reg A+ options.

SEC RULE 506(B) IN REGULATION D

Deals under Rule 506(b) are sometimes called "private placements." With a 506(b) deal, you can raise an unlimited amount of money and sell shares to an unlimited number of accredited investors. The number of non-accredited investors is capped at 35e. Yes, that is correct. You are only allowed to accept up to 35 non-accredited, sophisticated passive investors into this type of offering. As Danny said earlier, those non-accredited investors must attest that they have enough experience with business and investments to understand the risks and benefits of the deal.

Because a 506(b) deal involves non-accredited investors, the SEC does not allow you to advertise it or solicit business from the general public. In order to demonstrate that there was no general solicitation, you need to have a documented prior existing substantive relationship with each individual investor.

There's no clear definition of what "substantive" means in this regulation. There are a few things that it clearly doesn't mean. For example, you can't advertise your deal offering on traditional or social media and sign up people from the general public who respond. You can't advertise the deal at all. It also means that you can't bring in investors with whom you've only had a single contact. There must be multiple touch points in the relationship. The regulation doesn't specify exactly how many, but more than one. You also must be in a position to evaluate the investor's financial circumstances and sophistication to know whether they are an accredited or non-accredited investor.

I recommend new operators start out working with 506(b) projects for two reasons: newer operators tend to start out with smaller deals, and because you're not advertising publicly, you can build your network of investors gradually while you learn the business. By including non-accredited investors, you can avoid dealing with third-party verification on accredited investors (which we'll discuss further below).

SEC RULE 506(C) IN REGULATION D

All of our new offerings are organized under Rule 506(c). With this structure, you can only work with accredited investors, and those investors must be verified by a third party (see the Resources section in the Toolkit for a list of the companies that we recommend). You can now advertise the deal publicly, and you don't need to demonstrate a prior relationship. You can still raise an unlimited amount of money from an unlimited number of accredited investors. You just can't bring on any non-accredited investors, whether they are sophisticated or not.

Another thing to keep in mind is that you should still use your investor relations process to build a relationship with these accredited investors even though the SEC says you don't have to. We don't build relationships just because the SEC thinks it's a good idea. We do it because people will only invest with someone that they trust, so you must build that relationship in order to find long-term success in raising capital.

All these requirements are built into our investor-relations process. If you follow the system, you will build actual substantive relationships with potential passive investors that can become long-term, mutually beneficial partnerships. You'll also have the documentation that you did everything by the book. I'll walk you through the elements of our 5-step system in Chapter 4.

Individual investors aren't the only place to find capital for your projects. You can also raise capital from institutional investors, which is a whole different ball game.

The Coveted Institutional Equity Investor

Let me disclose up front that we don't use institutional equity in our deals. Our goal is to take multifamily assets out of the hands of institutions and make them accessible to private investors. So I can tell you all about it, but be warned, it's coming through my own philosophical and strategic lens.

Institutional investors are entities that invest money on behalf of their members or clients and have a large amount of capital to deploy—to the extent that they get preferential treatment in your deals. We're talking about banks, pension funds, hedge funds, endowments, insurance companies, and similar enterprises. Institutional investors like large multifamily assets because of their stability and robust returns, and they will often place capital with several different operating groups.

Besides our goal of putting multifamily properties into private hands, there are a number of pragmatic reasons that we don't take on institutional-level capital. First, it's more expensive and would take away more from our bottom line as operators. For example, a typical profit-sharing structure with private equity might be a 70/30 split, with 70% going to the investors and 30% to the operators. Institutional investors are more likely to demand a 90/10 split, or maybe even a 95/5 split.

There are also more strings attached to these larger checks. Institutional investors will want clawback clauses and take-back rights. They require more reporting and more detailed analysis, from the proforma to the budget and the goals. They're generally more of a pain to deal with than your private investors. As the 500-pound gorilla at the negotiating table, institutional investors are used to getting their own way. Ultimately, we don't have to sacrifice our share of the profits to work with institutional equity because we just don't need it. We already have more than enough private investors to acquire the deals we want.

When you're starting out as an operator, institutional capital usually isn't an option for you. Institutional investors want to see a track record, typically three to five years with full-cycle deals and strong returns, before investing in a new operating group. So in the beginning, I'd advise you not to worry about it at all. It's really a big waste of your time until you've built your track record.

As you grow, institutional capital may become an option for you to consider. And you may have a deal where you decide it's the best option. This is something that you may at some point in the future consider on a deal-by-deal basis. But I'd never want to rely on it exclusively.

Putting Theory into Practice

Now that you understand the concepts behind the Investor Triad and why they matter, I want to walk you step-by-step through our process. We began building this process early on in our business, and I encourage you to start using it from Day 1. We rely on a lot of technology and some specialized staff members to execute the steps, but you can start small and scale up. The process works no matter what tools you use. Let's get started.

Chapter 4

Five Steps to Successful Investor Relations

Dan Handford

In the beginning, on our very first deal, we encountered the most stressful time we've ever had in raising capital. You can't ask investors to put money into a deal that doesn't exist yet, so you have to find, underwrite, and bid on a property *before your investors have committed their capital.* Once you're in the process of acquiring a property, you are on a hard deadline. Everything has to move fast. You don't have time to scratch your head and wonder if you know anyone with money. You must have your network of potential investors in place before you bid on a deal.

We learned that the hard way. We found a deal, but we didn't have enough investors. We were working phone calls every single day, pounding the pavement to meet with people, trying to find the money. It took us the full sixty days of the contract period to raise the last bit of the money we needed—and it was only $2.5 million. Back then, that was a huge amount of money to us. (Of course, it's still a lot of money, but now we're usually raising $20 million to $40 million on a deal.)

We were in crisis mode. We realized that we needed a system in place to properly attract new investors and have them ready to invest on our next deal. Nobody wants to be in a position where they make an offer on a property and then say, "Oh crap!" When you're putting in offers, you need the confidence that you'll have the equity needed to close and be ready on time with minimal hassle. If you're freaking out, you won't be able to be as aggressive in winning the bid for the property, and you probably won't win very many deals.

Now we've developed a system that allows us to find qualified investors, build trust, manage our relationships with them, and keep their trust long-term by delivering on our promises. I'm going to share this system with you so you can stay out of "Oh, crap!" mode, for good.

We built this process by watching people do it the wrong way. We refined it by applying it in our own syndication business. I'm sharing it with you because it works. In this system, you'll move potential investors through the steps of the Investor Triad: Know, Like, and Trust, and then continue nurturing that relationship for the long term. The process consists of 5 stages as shown in the diagram below: raising capital, building relationships, securing capital, ongoing communications, and winning referrals.

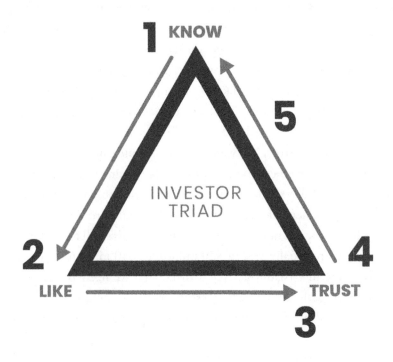

Step 1: Raising Capital

The first step to raising capital is finding investors—that means finding people who have the money and interest to invest. In this phase, you're attracting people and making yourself known. At the same time, you want to be known for the right reasons, so you want to elevate yourself into a position of credibility where investors can have confidence in you.

Becoming an Expert

One of the ways you can put yourself out there is by building an authority platform. Our group, the *Multifamily Investor Nation* (MFIN), gives us an expert position relative to the investor. When new people find us, they immediately see us as the leaders of this group, and that gives us a position of authority. We focus on putting out weekly content to educate the community on how to do multifamily investing.

This does not mean that you only have to be an authority in the real estate or multifamily space. You could also become an authority in another field like business, marketing, or another professional field where you could demonstrate your expertise.

Conferences: In-person or Virtual

You could organize your own virtual or in-person conference. Our MFIN group has been hosting a virtual conference twice a year since January 2019, and this platform allows us to attract a lot of potential investors into our fold. We also host our in-person, annual Multifamily Investor Nation Convention (MFINCON) once a year in June, with special celebrity guests such as Shaquille O'Neal, Barbara Corcoran, Jocko Willink, Alex Rodriguez, and Robert Cialdini.

Now you may be thinking, "How do I attract *passive* investors by teaching *active* investors how to start or improve their own syndication business? Wouldn't that just create more competition for me?"

I hear that question frequently, but it's based on a couple of misconceptions. First, there are a lot of investors who think they want to become operators, but when they find out how much work it actually entails to run a successful syndication business, they change their minds. They prefer to invest with someone else—and that someone else is our group, since we have been teaching them.

The second point is that there is a great deal of collaboration in the apartment syndication space. Many well-known syndicators invest with us passively through their self-directed IRAs or 401ks, since they are not allowed to invest in their own deals. They want to invest with someone that they know, like, and trust. Our authority platform MFIN helps us get to know most of the trustworthy syndicators in the space and build relationships with them, so they want to invest with us when the time comes. We reciprocate with many of these well-known syndicators and invest with them as well.

If you don't want to host your own conference, you could seek out speaking opportunities at conferences, which would still give you status and credibility as an expert in the space.

Podcasting: Host Your Own or Be a Guest

You could host your own podcast or be a guest on someone else's podcast. We host our own podcast called the *Multifamily Investor Nation*, where we only interview active investors who are closing real multifamily deals. In order to be a guest, the investor must have closed a multifamily deal with 5 or more units in the last 12 months.

The hardest part about starting your own podcast is to come up with a unique name and topic, because so many topics have already been done in the podcasting space. Don't let a desire to differentiate yourself hold you back, though—all you are trying to do is create a platform where you are the authority. Of course, you want to market your podcast and get the word out, but your visibility will increase with time as you interview high-level guests. You would be surprised how easy it is to message these experts and invite them to be on your podcast, and how willing they are to spend the time with you, not to mention how much valuable promotion you'll receive when they promote their episode to their own network of contacts.

If you have knowledge or expertise in another area, like business or marketing, it's a great idea to seek out guest slots on podcasts or channels related to that topic instead of ones devoted to multifamily or real estate. You can talk about your prior experience and then introduce your new business venture in apartment syndication.

Think Outside the Box

I always prefer to be the only one in the room looking for capital instead of competing for attention with the host or other speakers. It's like going to an in-person real estate conference or meetup. They can be good for networking with other operators, but they aren't great for finding investors. Everyone's there looking for the same thing, so the few investors that show up get mobbed like fat rats on a Cheeto.

In my town, we have an executive club with membership by invitation only. Once you're in, you can network with other high-level executives. In an atmosphere like that, you'll probably be the only one looking for capital—but you don't want to be too pushy. Remember, you're there to build relationships, not be a pest. Ask people what they do. Have a conversation. Eventually they'll ask what you do, and you'll tell them. If they're interested, they'll want to join you. You don't have to do any hard selling because successful people can recognize a good opportunity on their own.

Another way to find investors is by speaking at conferences. If you're just getting started, you might wonder how (or why) you could get to speak onstage. I'm telling you, there are always opportunities. For example, you could moderate a panel discussion—that's a great way to look like an expert, when really you're the one asking questions of the experts.

Finding these opportunities is all about reaching out and getting in contact with event organizers. Offer to help with any panels they may be doing, let them know you'll ask any questions they want, and make the speakers look good. Organizers always need reliable help. It gets you in front of people so they can know who you are.

Your authority platform might be a bit different than ours. Some people offer mentoring or coaching. You might write a book. You might become a guest on other people's podcasts or YouTube channels. No matter what elements you include in your platform, make sure you're offering accurate, useful information. Otherwise, you won't keep that authority for long.

Once people know who you are, you need to stay in contact and build a relationship that moves them from the Knowing phase to the Liking phase.

Version One is Better Than Version None

This is one of my favorite quotes, and I remind myself of it almost everyday. Don't get stuck in analysis paralysis. Pick one of these avenues to meet investors. Start something small and simple. You can scale it up as you go, but the most important thing you need to do is *start*. Get the first version out and then develop and perfect it. You learn from experience and feedback, so your first version will never be the best version. The only way to reach the best version is by creating the early version and putting it out there.

Step 2: Building Relationships

If the first stage of this process is getting introduced, the second phase is courting. You need to engage with your prospective investors and spend some quality time with them so they can get to know you better.

One mistake I see a lot of new operators make is that they just *collect* contacts but don't *connect* with them. They'll try a lot of different ways to attract new investors and compile a huge list of prospects. Then they don't have a deal right away, so they just throw all those names on an email list. They might send out an email blast once a month, but they don't really have much communication with their investors between deals. Soon those contacts go cold because there wasn't any human connection. You don't want a potential investor to forget who you are and toss your emails in the spam folder!

Once a new investor opts into our community, we reach out to them with personalized communication as well as regular updates about our projects. Now let's dive into some specific techniques to cultivate these relationships.

By Phone

We ask new investors to formalize our connection through an intake form on our website. As soon as they hit "submit" on that form, one of the members of our investor relations team will call them on the phone to introduce themselves. If they can't reach the person for any reason, they'll leave a voicemail thanking the investor for filling out the form and inviting them to schedule time on their calendar to talk. If they can't reach them by phone, they'll send a personal email and try to set up a call later. The goal is to deepen the relationship.

Whether they have the initial conversation right away or later on, they follow certain talking points to make sure we're really getting to know that investor's goals, their financial picture, and their risk tolerance. As I mentioned earlier, this type of screening is a regulatory requirement for a 506(b) but not a 506(c). Regardless of the regulation, getting to know your investors is a common-sense, human requirement for building a relationship. So I recommend that you have these calls with everyone.

You can see an example call script in our Apartment Syndication Toolkit at PassiveInvesting.com/Toolkit.

I never want my investors to feel like they're just a number. I want to have open communication with them so they feel like we're creating an actual relationship. That's why we always give out our direct cell phone numbers and our direct email addresses. We rarely get contacted by investors, but we want to make sure they know that if they need one of us, we aren't hiding behind a faceless website with a no-reply bulk email address. I want them to be confident that they're dealing with real people, and they have access to us. That's how you build credibility and trust over time.

Once our investor relations person has had an initial phone conversation, the investor gets added to our passive investor club. First, we add their contact information to our Customer Relationship Management (CRM) software. We also program them into our phones and send them a quick text greeting. That text includes a V-card with all of our contact information. That way, we know one of us is programmed into their phone. If they do contact us later with questions, we can tell which of us contacted them initially.

In Person

When we add a new investor to our cell phones after the initial phone encounter, we use the "Company" field of the contact form to list the city and state where they're located. We also note the nearest large city or **metropolitan statistical area (MSA)**, since that's how we keep track of our projects and plan our travel.

For example, if an investor lives in Riverview, Florida, I know that the nearest large city we'd likely be traveling to is Tampa. They're in the Tampa MSA. Now, anytime I'm traveling to Tampa for an event or a property tour, I can search my phone and see which of our investors live nearby that I could reach out to. I can send them all a quick text message to set up a coffee date or possibly even a group dinner. When we have the opportunity, I love to arrange dinners for our investors to get together. It's a wonderful chance for us to meet, and for them to meet each other.

This type of personal contact is the "secret sauce" to deepening authentic relationships with investors. You can't fake personal attention, and you can't build a personal connection if all you do is toss them onto a mass email list. This system isn't about collecting the biggest number of emails. It's not called the "investor email process." It's the investor relationship process.

Snail Mail

In our CRM system, we capture the investor's physical mailing address from their intake form. We want to make sure we can communicate with them beyond phone and email. Our email list has a very high open rate—about 52% to 53%. Really, that's a phenomenal open rate. Marketers would kill or die for an open rate like that because a 15% to 20% open rate is considered excellent by email marketing standards and benchmarks. Our open rate is high because our email list is highly cultivated. These are people who have opted in, people we've had real phone conversations with, who are expecting these emails.

However, the idea that half our investors aren't reading our emails just didn't sit right with me. It made me think, "What gets a near 100% open rate?" Paper mail. So we put the effort in—instead of just hitting "send" on an email campaign, somebody physically gets it into our mailbox, puts the flag up, and off it goes.

The first week of every month, like clockwork, we send a printed, physical newsletter. It gives us another real-world touchpoint outside the internet, and we make sure it's worth opening and reading. It's a high-gloss print booklet, usually about 12 to 16 pages long. The investors get to hear from each partner and our team members about how we think and how we operate. We talk to them about any upcoming changes in our business model, strategy, or plans so they aren't blindsided by it.

We also make the newsletter interactive and include the investors' families. We'll take a photo of one of our apartment communities, convert it into a coloring page, and include it in the newsletter. It's the first thing my kids ask for when the newsletter shows up in the mail. And of course, then it ends up on the refrigerator (with our PassiveInvestor.com branding on it). Then it becomes a conversation piece. We'll take some of the words from the prior month's newsletter and create a word-search puzzle. If they do the puzzle and send it in, we'll put them into a prize drawing for something nice, like a $50 Amazon gift card. We make the newsletter into an activity they can pass around, discuss, enjoy, and respond to. Those entries in the drawing let us know that they're engaging with us.

You can see an example of our newsletter in our Apartment Syndication Toolkit at PassiveInvesting.com/Toolkit.

I'm sure some of our investors open the newsletter, glance at it, and toss it in the recycle bin. That's fine. They opened it. It's still a touchpoint. They got it out of the mailbox, saw our name and branding, and they're thinking of us every single month.

If an investor joins us in the middle of the month and missed the newsletter mailing, we'll make a point of letting them know on the initial phone call that we have some extra copies, and we'll drop one in the mail so they can start receiving our investor communications. They love that, and again, it's one more touch point.

When we open up a new deal for investment, we publish an investor offering memorandum that outlines the property and the terms of the deal. We have them designed and laid out to the same standard as our print newsletters so they look sharp and professional. We want to make sure that all our investors know about new opportunities, even if they aren't great about opening email. We've also found that people take a lot of pride in these offering documents as keepsakes or trophy pieces. They like to show them off to their family, friends, and colleagues: "Look what I own!" We make sure they can show them off proudly.

You can see an example offering memorandum in our Apartment Syndication Toolkit at PassiveInvesting.com/Toolkit.

When we started out, we couldn't afford a professionally designed, full-color booklet on glossy paper. We started with something simple.

We hired a freelancer on one of the gig platforms like Upwork.com, and they put a template together for us. We worked our way up from there, and now we have an in-house designer. That's how you build a business like this—execute on the principles of good relationship building, and the external details will get more sophisticated over time.

Email

Email certainly has a place in your overall communication strategy. After you bring that new investor into your network, you should email them an example investor offering memorandum, so they can understand what some of your prior deals looked like. If you're just starting out and you don't have a finalized deal to present, you can get ideas from other groups and create an example of your ideal project. There's nothing deceptive about this—make sure that it's clear this is an example of what a similar deal might look like. This helps them understand the business, if they're new, and helps them understand your philosophy and investing strategy.

You might want to develop a company pitch deck that you can email to your investors. This is a brochure to introduce the concept of passive apartment investing, as well as introducing your business. You'd include information about your company, your track record of performance, the partners, why apartments are a good investment, and the trends that have shown strong performance over 15, 20, or 30 years.

You can see an example of a company pitch deck in our Apartment Syndication Toolkit at PassiveInvesting.com/Toolkit.

You might include your business plan, the criteria you use in choosing projects, and your projected returns. This pitch deck could also incorporate a sample offering memorandum. We use our pitch deck very sparingly because most of our investors are already familiar with passive investing when they come to us. It can be a beneficial tool to educate first-time passive investors.

You should also send out regular updates about the business. We email our investors a monthly report that repurposes articles from our print newsletter. Reusing content is a practical strategy to make your system easier to manage. If you had to write and lay out two completely separate publications every month, that would take up way too much of your time. However, we always delay repurposing content by at least 30 to 60 days because we want our print newsletter to have the freshest material. Email is useful, but we really place the highest priority on live communications and physical documents because they carry the most weight in relationship building.

The more touch points you have with your investors during this courting phase, the stronger your relationship will be. Via phone, snail mail, email, and in-person contact, each of those touch points will help move your investors around the investor triad from Like to Trust.

Step 3: Securing Capital

This is the stage where you get your investors to commit to investing in your deal and transfer funds into the project's bank account. You have to be proactive about executing this step. You've spent so much time and effort attracting and courting investors, I assume you're going to do a phenomenal job and have hundreds, if not thousands of investors ready to open their bank account and invest in your next deal. Now you have to walk them through a process of securing that investment.

Unfortunately, I've seen so many people fail to take enough initiative at this stage. I've called up other operators literally two weeks before closing and asked, "So, how much money have you raised at this point?"

They'll say, "Oh, we have it all raised. It's all committed."

Then I ask, "How much is in the bank account?"

"Oh, none of it!" they answer. "We've talked to them and they've verbally committed to invest."

I keep asking, "Do you have all their documents signed?"

"No, not yet."

Two weeks before closing? They might be raising 7 or 8 million dollars, and none of it is in the bank yet? These are the folks who don't stay in the business for long. They get caught with their pants down, and they lose deals because they don't have the capital in place on time. They lose their reputation with brokers and sellers because they couldn't deliver on the contract. They lose their reputation with investors because they have to give all the money back. They wasted everyone's time and they're sunk. It's hard to recover from that.

The process of securing capital correctly will allow you to continue to grow. Most people are process-oriented. They want to be guided and have their hand held when they're doing something important or complicated. When an investor says they want to invest in your deal, you need to walk them through everything they need to do. So let's walk you through that now.

Project Funding Timeline

Your timeline for securing capital revolves around 2 key dates: the date you close on the asset (set by agreement with the seller) and the funding date (set by you). In these types of transactions, it's common for the closing date to be fluid. There are so many variables that can change at the last minute, you can expect that sometimes the closing may be delayed a day or two. Now, you and I know that's normal. The investors may not realize it's normal, so you don't want to give them an exact date in advance, in case they feel panicky when it shifts. With so much to do around the closing, there's no point sending out a bunch of nonessential updates about routine schedule changes. Therefore, it's best to communicate your closing date as a week-long range. For example, "Closing: week of August 10th."

Your funding date is different, as it should be a firm date. This needs to be a very clear deadline. Set your funding date 3 to 4 weeks before your closing. That will keep you from getting caught with your pants down like our unfortunate friends in the earlier example. Having this set 3–4 weeks prior to closing allows you enough time to get additional capital if you are falling short. You don't want to wait until the week of closing, as this might be too late to fill any equity gaps that could prevent you from closing. It also gives you some breathing room to back out of the deal if you absolutely have to. If your funding date is correctly timed, you will know before the end of the due diligence period whether or not you will have the funds to close. If you have to back out at that point, you hopefully won't lose all your earnest money.

Once you have those dates set, you can start introducing your investors to the deal and guiding them through the process.

INTRODUCE THE DEAL

The day we have the PSA inked, we send an email to all our investors with highlights of the deal. This includes projected returns, the general timeline, and a description of our reasoning as to why we like this deal. We include a link so they can download the offering memorandum (as mentioned in the Relationship Building phase). This initial email also contains two important action steps for the investor: we invite them to a webinar where we will discuss the deal, and we invite them to submit a soft reserve.

Samples of offering documents and other project documentation are available in our Apartment Syndication Toolkit at PassiveInvesting.com/Toolkit.

A soft reserve is a nonbinding commitment to participate in the project. It lets the investors "save their spot" in the deal by letting us know their interest and the amount they intend to invest. It's their RSVP. They submit their soft reserve through a form on our website, which also asks them to grade themselves on a scale of 1 to 10 on how likely they are to invest.

The soft reserve has both psychological and practical benefits for you as the operator. If you have a solid group of investors and a good deal to present, the available shares in the project will fill up quickly.

That encourages investors to act on their decision and not dillydally. After all, if they change their mind or don't like the final terms when it's time to sign the legal documents, they aren't bound by the soft reserve. Further, making a written commitment carries more weight than a verbal agreement on a phone call. People put more thought into filling out the form than they would into casually saying, "Sure, I'm in." There will still be some who don't follow through, but you can have a higher degree of confidence in the written commitment. Finally, the soft reserves give you a short list of people to follow up with if they lag behind on completing the next steps.

As soon as an investor submits a soft reserve, they're added to a spreadsheet so we can track the amount of money they committed, how they ranked their intention to invest, whether they registered for the webinar, and their progress through the other steps. We use a software called AirTable. You could also use Excel or something similar. After submitting, they receive an invitation to join our investor management portal. This portal will allow us to send and receive secure documents for signature later on.

THE WEBINAR

Three to five days after the introductory email, we host a webinar to present the deal to our investors. Everyone who responded to the initial email to register gets an invitation link. In the webinar, we encourage them again to submit a soft reserve. More people register for the webinar than actually attend, but the registrations give us a hot list of interested investors to follow up with.

We also record the webinar, and email it to the entire list of investors. That way, people have another opportunity to watch the video on their own time. Our email software also allows us to track which investors clicked on the link to watch the recording so they can be added to the hot list. We use a CRM software called Active Campaign, but there are a number of CRM services with similar functions.

People today are more visually oriented than ever before. The current generation of investors grew up not just with television, but with iPads and smartphones. They want a visual connection with people they're going to do business with. You will gain more credibility and trust from your investors if they can see you as a real person, talking to them directly. Even when we're playing a slideshow or screen-sharing during a webinar, we leave our cameras on so the investors can see us picture-in-picture. The personal connection makes all the difference.

THE PRIVATE PLACEMENT MEMORANDUM

Four or five business days after the webinar, we release the **Private Placement Memorandums (PPMs)** for the committed investors to review. We try to move quickly on releasing these documents, because we find that our investors are eager to get the paperwork done, and they'll ask for it if it doesn't arrive pretty soon. You'll probably need to stay on top of your securities attorney to make sure they meet your timelines.

The PPM consists of in-depth information about the operator, the asset, the terms of the deal, risk disclosures, and projected returns, as well as the legal documents that investors must sign in order to participate. That includes the Subscription Agreement that defines the terms of their investment, the Operating Agreement that governs their membership in the SPE, and an Investor Suitability questionnaire. Along with the PPM, the investors receive wiring instructions to send in their funds.

You can download a sample PPM as part of our Apartment Syndication Toolkit, at PassiveInvesting.com/Toolkit.

We distribute these documents in bulk via DocuSign through our online investor portal. DocuSign verifies that the investors have re-viewed the documents and manages the electronic signatures. When an investor completes the DocuSign process, we send them a confirmation email: "Congratulations, we received your PPM and you've been accepted into the deal. Now it's time to wire your funds. Make sure you wire them in by the deadline." We also let them know that we'll confirm receipt of the wire transfer within 24–48 hours.

FUNDING

When we form the SPE that will own the property, we set up bank accounts for that entity. The wiring instructions that accompany the PPM direct the funds into the SPE's bank account so they will be available for closing.

Once an investor signs off on the legal documents, their funds are due. When we see that the wire transfer was received, we email a confirmation to the investor. All this communication is important for the investor because they're sending a lot of money. We try to confirm back to them the same day, to ensure that nothing goes wrong. Occasionally, you might not see the wire transfer show up for 2 days. That's stressful for everyone, because naturally the investor will worry about where their money is and what happened to it! Staying in close contact with your investors during the funding period ensures everyone can get a good night's sleep.

So you've moved your investors around the triad from Know, through Like, to Trust. They demonstrated that trust by placing their money into your project. Now that you've won their trust, you have to keep it, with an ongoing commitment to reliability and transparency in the way you communicate with your investors after the deal is done.

Step 4: Postdeal Communications

After they invest in a project, the members of your investor club should continue to receive all the regular communications we discussed in step two on building relationships. They should also receive updates and information specific to the deal they're invested in.

Property Reports

First, we send our investors a monthly email report on the performance of the asset for the previous month. For example, the report sent on February 14 covers the asset's performance in January. The report includes occupancy status, preleased occupancy, marketing updates like changes to the branding, updates on renovation projects to the interior and exterior, and anything else relevant to the physical asset. It also covers the financial performance of the asset: how well we're executing our business plan and whether our revenues are on target.

The report may also contain not-so-good news. If there was a fire on the property, or storm damage, we inform the investors and give them context to understand how it will affect the asset financially. If there was a drop in occupancy, we discuss the causes and what we can do to mitigate it.

These reports keep us continually engaged with our investors. That engagement gives them confidence and a level of comfort that their money is in good hands. The updates also let us set reasonable expectations about the property's performance, particularly around how any ups or downs with the property might affect their monthly cash flow distributions.

Distributions

Every month, the investors receive their cash distribution by direct deposit. Our target date is to have the deposit drop on the 20th of the month. This means every month when the investor reconciles their bank statement, they'll see cash flow coming in and make a positive connection to us.

Most operating groups do quarterly distributions instead of monthly. It saves a bit of work and a little bit of money, but the downside of quarterly distributions is that you only get that contact point with your investor 4 times a year instead of 12 times a year. You have established a relationship with your investors, but that doesn't mean it's time to slack off strengthening that relationship! You want your investors to stay with you long-term, so that means you want to keep engaging with them long-term.

I often hear other syndicators complain that monthly distributions are more expensive than quarterly. I don't really understand that complaint. The direct deposits through ACH aren't free, but they're cheap as can be. It costs us less than $50 a month to process distributions to all the investors in a deal. If a deal is so tight that you can't afford $50 in administrative fees a month, you shouldn't get into that deal in the first place.

Monthly distributions take some time, but again, it's not much time. Our investor portal keeps track of everything for us. We press a button, the portal spits out a listing called a NACHA report (the National Automated Clearing House Association). We upload the NACHA file to the bank, the bank processes it in 2 to 3 days, and the money is transferred from the SPE's account to the investors. Technology makes these things quick and simple, but there's no more valuable touch point in your investor relationship than those regular cash flow deposits.

Financial Statements

Once a quarter, we release the financials of the property so investors can get hard numbers on the property's performance. The main statement is the T-12, or the trailing twelve months financial report. The T-12 lists all the income and expenses, representing the net operating income, over the past 12 months. We also release the current rent roll so the investors can verify that the occupancy and other figures are correct.

We don't email these documents out. We upload them to the investor portal and notify the investors in that month's regular report that the financials are available. So in April, July, October, and January we alert them that the financial statements for the last quarter are ready to download.

Tax Documents

Once a year, we produce a Schedule K-1 for each investor. The K-1 is a federal tax document that lists the individual investor's share of the income, losses, credits, and deductions for the business. The investors need this document in order to correctly file and pay their taxes. Our goal is to release the K-1s by the 15th of March. Some years we get them out a couple of weeks earlier, some years they might be a day or two later, but always striving to get them out by the end of March. That gives our investors time to do their own filings.

Tax documentation should be very straightforward for your investors. Unfortunately, it can also be a source of great frustration if an operator drags their feet and doesn't deliver on time. When a K-1 is delayed, the investors may need to file extensions on their personal or business tax returns, and it causes a lot of unnecessary angst. If there is a delay for any reason, make sure you communicate with your investors so they understand the timeline. Don't make them chase you.

If you make your investors' lives more complicated or frustrating, they aren't likely to invest with you again or refer anyone else. This step makes that big of an impact, so you must keep on top of your CPA to ensure you send out your K-1s on time. One thing that we have learned about the end of the year tax timing is that CPAs are always busy during this time of the year, so it is wise to spread out your tax preparation work to multiple firms. This will help you maintain the goal of releasing the K-1s by the end of March as you continue to grow your company and the number of tax filings begin to grow.

Everything you do from getting to know investors, to building relationships, developing trust and rewarding that trust, all bring you to the point where it's time to start traveling around the investor triad again. This time, you'll be getting to know people that your investors referred to you.

Step Five: Asking for Referrals

The coolest referrals are the ones you don't even have to ask for. Often, our investors will send friends and family to us unsolicited. We love that! Word of mouth is the gold standard, the best advertising you can have. When you have raving fans, it's proof that you're doing something right.

The downside of unsolicited referrals is that you never know when they're coming in, and you can't always rely on them. At some point you have to figure out ways to ask for them.

Now, some businesses will ask their customers straight-up, "Will you give me the name and number of five friends I can call and talk about what we do?" I've never liked that. To me, that's always felt awkward and pushy. It works for some people, but to me it doesn't sound appealing: "Hey, I just wheedled your name and number out of your friend, so I'm calling to see if you have enough money to invest."

It's just weird. They aren't that different from cold leads. Theoretically, it was a "referral" but you basically stiff-armed your investor to get those names. I prefer to be a little more strategic.

Newsletters

One method we use about twice a year is to send out extra copies of the print newsletter. We'll include a shrink-wrapped extra copy in their mailer, with a sticker encouraging the investor to share it with family, friends, or colleagues. Remember, these are high-quality, high-engagement pieces that people really enjoy. They don't want to give away their own copy, so now they have an extra to pass along. By making the effort to print up and send an extra copy, you get them thinking about who they might give it to, whether that's at the office, at church, at the club, or wherever they are. Most of your investors will have people in their sphere of influence with money to invest, but they may not know how to start a conversation about investing. That physical newsletter opens the conversation for them.

After they've invested with us, and they're happy with the returns, sharing the opportunity with others lets them be the hero. Instead of asking them to give up their friends' contact information, you're giving them something tangible to share. And you don't have to make any cold calls to introduce yourself. The investor, someone the recipient already knows, likes, and trusts, is doing the talking for you.

Investor Dinners

Back in step 2, I talked about arranging group dinners with local investors when we visit different markets around the country. They're great for building relationships, and they're also a great opportunity to get referrals. When we invite them, we ask if they're able to bring a friend who might be interested in investing.

Again, the investor is the one making contact in a very attractive and low-pressure way. Worst-case scenario, the friend is going to get a nice meal and a nice conversation with financially savvy people in their city—people they might want to get to know anyway. We don't do any kind of huge presentation or hard sales pitch at these dinners. It's all about sharing a nice meal at a nice restaurant and building deeper relationships with our investors.

I'll tell you right now, our investor relations system isn't the industry standard. There is no industry standard. I can also tell you that other operators call us up all the time, asking where we get our content or who designs our materials. I tell them it's all done in-house by our own designer, and they can't have her. But they're really missing the point.

The design work elevates everything, but it's not what attracts and keeps investors. The power is in the system. We're laying out our entire PassiveInvesting.com playbook here for you, and the system will work for anyone. The question is, are you willing to work the system?

Building on Your Foundation

You have the basic concepts of how apartment syndication works. You understand the benefits and why it's a great investment and a great business model. If you plan to become an operator yourself, you're on your way to building a network of eager, engaged investors. Now all you need is an apartment building to buy!

You're ready to move on to Part 2: Making Deals.

Part 2

Making Deals

You'll get the most out of this section if you're an active investor who intends to start an apartment syndication business of your own. However, if you're considering passive investing, you'll still get a great benefit from understanding asset classes, valuations, market analysis, and underwriting. These concepts will help you set your criteria for the type of deals you're looking for and the types of operators you want to invest with.

In this section, you'll learn:

- Chapter 5: Finding Deals
  - How to understand and set investing criteria for your operating group
  - How to value multifamily assets within the context of their local market
  - How to cultivate good working relationships with multifamily brokers

- Chapter 6: Analyzing Markets and Assets
  - Understanding and performing a detailed analysis of the fundamental economic indicators in a local market
  - Where to find the data you need to make this analysis
  - How to determine if a particular property will yield the returns you're looking for

- Chapter 7: Debt, Equity, and Deal Structuring
  - Finding the right lender
  - Securing a loan for your multifamily deal
  - Planning the cash flow returns for your investors
  - Structuring the capital and equity returns for your deal

- Chapter 8: Acquisitions
  - The bidding process in multifamily acquisitions
  - Winning strategies for negotiating with lenders
  - How to conduct due diligence and prepare to close the deal
  - How to present the deal to your investors
  - How to ensure your capital is in place for closing

Chapter 5

Finding Deals

Brandon Abbott

Focus. It's the key to success in any business, and apartment syndication is no different. There are so many multifamily assets out there, an operator can't possibly research them all or try to invest in them all. If you just set yourself the goal that you're going to find any multifamily asset anywhere, you'll get distracted and waste far too much time and energy running around without making any progress. You need to set criteria for the multifamily assets you want to operate.

Set Your Investing Criteria

At PassiveInvesting.com, we pursue B+ to A+ multifamily assets, built between 2000 and the current year, that need no renovation, light renovation, or moderate renovation. We look for properties in markets with population and job growth in specific geographic areas. The point is that by setting these parameters, we screen out a lot of things we don't want, making our decisions a lot easier. If we see a community built in 1994, we don't even look at it. If we get a 2005 community, but it's not in our target market, we don't even look. We're only investigating assets that fit our criteria in the markets we select.

Which category of property you buy has a big impact on your business plan because it dictates how much you'll spend on renovation and capital improvements, and how much upside you might have to increase revenue. Your criteria must include the age and condition of the property, the asset class, and your market. Let's start by defining terms.

Know Your Asset Classes

Multifamily properties are graded into four classes that reflect the value of the property and its potential profitability. It's a shorthand to express complicated factors like age, condition, location, quality standards, and amenities.

Class A properties are brand-new builds, 5–10 years old or less. They're located in a very good part of town where high-income earners would like to rent, and have popular, high-quality amenities. This category can go up to AA or even AAA+, which would be high-rises with penthouses, really the top of the market.

Class B assets are sometimes older, less than 20 years old. They are still in a good part of town, but not brand-new, trendy areas. They will have some amenities, but not the same type of high-end amenities as a Class A asset. They're in good shape with no deferred maintenance. The residents are what we call "gray-collar": some blue-collar, some white-collar. They're safe and pleasant places to live but not luxury properties.

Class C assets could be anywhere from 25 to 40 years old. They're in a rougher part of town where average rents are lower. They will have fewer amenities. The resident demographic is going to be drawn from the blue-collar workforce and has a more limited income. These residents tend to *need* to rent as opposed to B or A class residents who may choose to rent. There are typically more maintenance issues due to age and more of a need to update amenities and other aesthetics.

Class D assets are kind of a no-go zone. There's a common saying that D stands for Danger, Drugs, Dilapidated, Death, and Do Not

Buy. These are the worst of the worst assets. They're horrible properties. I'm talking about the kind of places where windows are getting smashed, and there's crime happening every day. People are getting killed. Nobody wants to live there, and nobody wants to buy them, either.

REPOSITIONING ASSETS

An interesting aspect of asset classes is that your geographic market also has classes that describe the different areas or neighborhoods. These market classes have the same type of grading scale from A to D. Since market classes don't factor in the specific features of one property, you sometimes find a difference between the property's asset class and market class. For example, you could have a B class asset in an A class area. That's a sweet spot because it gives you the opportunity to get a really great return since the property is undermanaged.

Sometimes it's possible to upgrade a property so much that you can move it into a higher asset class, say from a C class asset to a B class, or from a B class to an A minus. It's very challenging to pull off, but if done well it can raise the NOI and the value of the property tremendously. In order to reposition an asset, it's important to buy in a market one or two levels up from the class of the property itself—so a C class property has a chance of moving up to B if it's in a B (or better yet, an A) class area. You'd have a very hard time leveling a property higher than its surrounding area because you won't be able to get the residents that you want for that property.

The opposite could also happen, though. If you tried to buy a B class asset in a C class area, you might not be able to increase rents enough to recoup the cost of the renovations. That could keep you from performing on your business plan and delivering your projected returns to investors.

Of course, neighborhoods don't stay static forever. An area that's Class B may gradually slip into a C area over time, or a Class B or C area may gentrify. There are some upsides to investing in gentrifying areas, such as tax breaks. The federal Opportunity Zone program pushed this type of investment. However, it is difficult to make such an investment work in a syndication model because it takes so long for cash flow to catch up to the level you need it to be. We do not invest in these areas as a result. It's very important that you understand the relationship of asset class and market class when you're looking for good deals.

Stabilization

Within your A, B, or C asset class, you can also set criteria about the property's stabilization. Remember, a stabilized asset is one that has 90% occupancy for at least 3 months. This term can also be used to indicate whether an asset is providing its maximum revenue or has the potential to increase revenue. A property can be categorized as value-add, prestabilized, or stabilized.

A value-add property is one that needs renovating and updating, which will allow you to raise the rent and possibly reposition it into a higher asset class. Value-add properties are usually going to start out as class B or class C, and you always want to consider the class of the surrounding area to make sure you can attract residents at your target rents. Once the property has achieved the predetermined business plan in terms of rent premiums and necessary renovations, it is considered stabilized from an underwriting perspective.

Prestabilized properties are recently built and haven't filled up with residents yet, so the rent is discounted. You might buy in at 80% occupancy and then bring it the rest of the way up. Then, after it becomes stabilized, you can gradually raise the rents until you achieve your business model. Prestabilized properties will usually be Class A because they're brand-new.

A completely stabilized property is already producing enough revenue without a need for extensive renovations. You'd just buy it and take over the management, and possibly cut some expenses. Many times, the developer is focused on stabilizing the property in terms of occupancy and therefore they have left "meat on the bone" on rent premiums. You may be able to increase rents at renewal up to 25% or more from where the developer set them.

Valuing Multifamily Assets

As Danny mentioned in Chapter 2, the value of an apartment community isn't based on "comparables" in the same way that single-family homes are. Multifamily assets are valued based on their profit-making potential. The profitability of an asset depends on how much you pay for it, how much income it can generate, and how much you can sell it for. Comparables look not only at what properties traded for in comparison with their NOI, but also what rents are achievable in the market.

The first two pieces of that equation are expressed as a ratio called the **capitalization rate (or cap rate)**. The cap rate of a given asset is the NOI divided by the purchase price. Cap rate = NOI ÷ purchase price.

Since real estate values and rents tend to move together across a regional market, each market has an overall expected cap rate that you can use to estimate the profitability of a property in that area. A high cap rate means you're getting more "bang for your buck": more income for your purchase price. The higher the cap rate, the higher the cash yields. The lower the cap rate, the lower the cash yields. A low cap rate means you're getting less income relative to the purchase price. So, to a certain degree, "comparables" are a factor because the cap rate of the whole market influences the value of the asset. Cap rates are intangible. They are determined from knowing your market. You cannot base your valuations simply on internet data because the target moves more quickly than historical data is posted.

Let's look at an example: 2 complexes in the same town each have 150 units. One complex generates $500,000 in NOI, and the other only generates $250,000. Obviously one property is worth less than the other to an investor, even though they are the same size and in the same city. So how do you know if buying one of those complexes makes sense?

You'd look at the prevailing cap rate for the market, plug it into the equation, and do the math. Cap rate = NOI ÷ price. Therefore, price (or value) = NOI ÷ cap rate. You'd divide that $500,000 by the prevailing cap rate, and find the estimated price that would make the property worth buying. You can also estimate what the property will be worth after you renovate and upgrade it.

The most important factor is the cap rate when you sell the property: your exit cap rate. It determines the cap rate you're looking for when you buy the property (your entry cap rate). If you buy a property at a 4% cap, renovate and increase NOI, but demand in the submarket has gone down, that will affect your ability to sell. If the cap rate expands to 5%, then you have lost value. The increase in cap rate negated the increase in NOI, and you will not be able to exit the property profitably.

However, if you buy at a 4% cap and complete your business plan, and the cap rate has compressed to 3.5% when you're ready to sell, then you will make a great return. Higher demand for properties in a submarket compresses the cap rate. Compressed cap rates can provide a return even on a flat NOI. Therefore, if you buy at a cap rate that's too low for the market, you will have a hard time exiting at the same or lower cap rate. In other words, you paid too much for the property in the first place. We'll go into more detail on market cap rates below.

Choose Your Market

Geographic markets are defined by **MSAs** based on data drawn from the federal census. An MSA consists of a city and the nearby communities that are connected to it—a metro area, in layman's terms. In real estate, we rank these as primary and secondary markets, or possibly tertiary markets if you want to go further afield.

Primary markets would be the largest and most prosperous cities, like Atlanta, New York, Dallas, and Charlotte or Raleigh-Durham in North Carolina. Secondary markets would be one level removed, like Greensboro and Wilmington in North Carolina, or Columbia and Charleston in South Carolina. Tertiary markets are markets that most people have never heard of, unless they live in the state or near the area.

When you consider a specific MSA to invest in, look at the statistical data to see if you can make a good return in that location. You want to see economic development happening, new businesses opening, and job growth. Look for the presence of blue-chip, publicly traded corporations. Businesses like that provide stable jobs that support the local economy. Another important statistic is median household income, but even more than the level of income, you want to see growth in the median income. All sorts of useful information is available at census. gov to give you a clear picture of which communities are growing and which are stagnant or struggling.

To find an area that will give you a good return, look for median income that exceeds three times the average rent you'll charge once you have completed your business plan. If the median income is less than three times your target average rent, there is a good chance that your resident base cannot afford your projected rents. Population growth is another big factor in choosing a market. You do not want to invest in an area with a declining population. The more people that are moving to an area, the more demand there will be for apartments. The more demand there is, the higher rents you can charge.

MARKET CAPITALIZATION RATES

The primary markets—the bigger, more expensive cities—have the lowest cap rates. As you move out into secondary and tertiary markets, demand for real estate goes down, so the cap rates go up. In areas with lower demand, the investment is more risky, but it has a relatively higher cash return for the investor. In a sense, sellers are offering a premium to entice investors to buy.

Some mentors and coaches encourage new operators to chase high cap rates: 9%, 10%, 11%, or 12% cap rate markets. In the short term, those high rates may translate into higher cash-on-cash returns, but in the long term there's a big hole in this strategy. It leaves out the third factor in the profitability equation: *how much you can make when you sell.*

Our strategy is to choose properties in primary markets with low cap rates. These properties have very strong demand—there might be 30 to 50 different operating groups bidding to acquire them. That demand compresses the cap rate for the market. But that's okay! We consider those lower cap rates to be a litmus test for how strong and stable the market actually is.

Let me give you an illustration. We'll compare a property in a 5% cap rate market with one in an 8% cap rate market. We'll say that the original purchase price of the property is $10 million, and the original NOI is $5 million.

I take that property in the 5% cap rate market and do the work to improve its NOI. I do renovations, I add amenities, I increase the rent, I cut expenses, and I wind up increasing the NOI by $100,000 per year. What does that do to the market value?

Do the math with me. Cap rate = NOI ÷ value, right? Therefore, value = NOI ÷ cap rate. We increased the NOI by $100,000, and the cap rate is 5%. So $100,000 ÷ 0.05 = $2 million. The property is now worth $12 million.

Look at the same scenario in the 8% cap rate market. I put in the same energy, the same effort, the same cost of renovations, and increase the NOI by the same amount, $100,000 per year. Now I do the same math: $100,000 ÷ 0.08 = $1.25 million. The property is now worth $11.25 million. The change in NOI produced a much smaller change in the property's value.

Now, the difference between increasing the value by $1.25 million and $2 million is $750,000. That may not sound enormous on a $10 million property. But remember, those margins are where the operator earns their keep. You are putting in the same amount of work and getting the same effect. Wouldn't you rather get paid more for it?

By investing in a lower cap rate market, you get far greater benefit from your improvements when you sell. You might get lower cash flows initially, but you have higher exit potential because of the way you can grow the value of the property in a lower cap rate environment.

Focus on People

Your best resource for finding markets, finding properties, and finding out the information you need to know is the people who know your market: property managers, other operators, and most of all, brokers. All major transactions at our level of the multifamily business go through brokers. Unlike in single-family purchases where you might have a seller's agent and a buyer's agent, with multifamily there is one broker who represents the property and acts as an intermediary between the two sides.

If you want to find deals, you need relationships with brokers—and if you want good deals, you need good relationships. As we mentioned in Chapter 1, real estate is a relational business. You need to establish strong relationships with a variety of brokers in your target market so they know who you are as a group. They need to have confidence in your ability to close on a deal so they know that you aren't just a tire-kicker wasting their time. Brokers have a lot of influence on which potential buyers get awarded a deal, so it's important that they like you and want to do business with you.

When we were new to the business, we had a mindset that brokers should be thanking us for buying the properties they were listing. However, as our portfolio has grown, we've learned over and over how important these broker relationships can be, so we've become more and more intentional about celebrating deals with our brokers. We'll take them to dinner whenever we close on a property or send them a gift. We might take them golfing at a resort as a way of investing in our group. You must celebrate the wins and make everyone feel important in their role.

We make sure to reach out to the brokers in our network regularly, about twice a month, whether we're looking for a deal or not. These are just friendly check-ins to keep in touch—ask about the family, or about their trip to Cabo. You want to stay front-of-mind. That way when a deal comes up, they'll think of you. Often, when we do these routine check-ins, brokers will mention a new deal coming up that I might be interested in.

We visit our submarkets several times a year, and just like we mentioned having coffee or dinner with local investors, we'll also set up time to catch up with brokers that we've met or worked with before. We'll chat about trends in the market, new projects, and just refresh that personal connection. Elevating your broker relationships beyond a cold, transactional level will elevate your business as a whole.

The Right Brokers for the Right Deals

As you set your criteria for where you want to invest, you're also setting criteria for which brokers you want in your network. For example, if you want to buy in the Charlotte, North Carolina MSA, and you're looking for a B-class, value-add property, then there will be particular brokers who are handling that area and class of properties.

You might have some flexibility—like looking for stabilized or prestabilized Class As—but you don't want to leave it wide open to "anything for sale in Charlotte." You'll get inundated with things you don't want, and it just makes more work to sift through them all. Stay focused. That will help you narrow down which brokers to talk to.

If possible, you want to get to know brokers before they're offering you a deal. I recommend you look up brokers in your target market who handle the kind of property you want. For our example, you can simply Google "multifamily brokers in Charlotte," check out the types of properties they're representing, and make a short list. Reach out to them, tell them who you are and what you're looking for, and try to get a meeting with them.

You can also leverage your existing relationships with brokers in one market to meet brokers in a new market. When we started looking for properties in Texas, our first call was to our broker network in the Carolinas. All those firms have contingencies in Texas, but we didn't know the people in those offices. Rather than cold-call, I reached out to my local connections and asked for an introduction in the new target market. That way, I'm walking into those new relationships with a warm connection, and I don't have to start all my relationship building from square one.

I'll ask the new brokers to send me all their deals that might meet our criteria, and then we'll set up a trip to tour many sites in one fell swoop. We exert as large a presence as possible, and then the deals start flowing in. These tours can be grueling, especially when you're having basically the same conversation over and over about who you are and the kind of property you're looking for, but that's all part of building a new network.

Making the Right Impression

When you meet a new broker, they will be interviewing you more than you're interviewing them. There are many, many operating groups vying for good investment properties (as I mentioned, it's not unusual to see 30 to 50 groups bidding on a property). The brokers will want to know where your money is coming from and what your business model is like. Are you an institutional group? Are you a REIT, or are you a syndicator? (These designations are determined by the source of your equity.) Who are you and how long have you been in business? Finally, they'll want to know your criteria for investment properties.

These conversations are the crucial moments when you need to know your vocabulary, and the reason you need to practice in a different market before you approach brokers you might really want to work with. If a broker starts asking you about **bad debt** and **loss to lease**, what **IRR** you're looking for, or what **cash-on-cash** you're looking for, you'd better know what they're talking about and have an educated answer. Otherwise, they'll write you off and you'll lose ground.

In order to buy a multifamily property, you have to have the financial credentials to support the deal. To take out a commercial loan, lenders require that you have a guarantor or a group of managing partners with net worth equal to the loan value, and liquidity equal to 10% of the loan balance. That way, if anything goes wrong and the asset stops performing, you as the borrower will have enough reserves to keep paying the loan. You will also need to provide (or find) **at-risk capital**. At-risk capital is nonrefundable earnest money otherwise known as an earnest money deposit (EMD). Making your earnest money "hard" or nonrefundable early in the process can give you leverage over other potential buyers, but you can only do that if you can truly afford to risk that money.

Brokers will ask about these qualifications. They aren't going to spend time showing properties to someone that the lenders will reject, or someone who is in too weak of a bargaining position to close the deal. The best situation you could have is that you guarantee all your own debt and provide all your own at-risk capital. Not everyone can do that, so it puts you in a strong position if you can. If nobody in your operating group has the financial status to guarantee the loan, you can bring in a **key principal** or **guarantor** to do so. The guarantor would receive a percentage of the general partnership or a fixed fee in order to give that security.

Finally, brokers will want to know how much experience you have and how many properties you have bought. It can be very difficult to jump right into your first deal as an operator because you don't have any experience. That's why we recommended in Chapter 1 that you start out as a limited partner with another operating group. This allows you to show a track record of participating in multifamily deals and demonstrate that you know the ropes.

I also recommend you make an effort to present yourself in the most professional way possible. Remember, you will be representing a group of investors with millions of dollars on the line. When we started out, my personal car was a Chevy Malibu. It was a good, comfortable, reliable car with good gas mileage. But it didn't convey the impression that I could close a multimillion dollar deal, so when I was meeting with brokers, I'd rent something nicer. Better yet, if you have several meetings and several properties to tour, hire a car and driver for the day. It lets you focus on business instead of finding your way around, and it helps build up your business persona.

Above all, take your relationships with brokers seriously. Don't be flippant or reckless and put offers on every deal you see, or give a false impression that you're ready to move on a deal when you are not able to. When you say you'll buy a property, it needs to be approved on every level and you need to be ready to start signing papers and cutting checks. If you make a verbal commitment and then come back later saying, "My partner didn't agree," brokers will get frustrated because you wasted their time. They will remember this next time you are bidding on a deal with other groups. Build a good, solid reputation as someone who delivers on their word. Reputation is paramount to your success. Play the long game.

Fully Marketed Versus Off-Market Deals

When you get to know the brokers in your target submarket, they'll put you on their distribution list. When a new property comes on the market, the brokers will send out an email blast to let buyers know about the opportunity. A property that is listed with a broker and on the public market is known as **fully marketed**.

An **off-market** property isn't currently up for sale publicly. Maybe they don't want to go through a whole marketing process with all of its drawbacks from a timing perspective. It's also always possible that an owner might consider selling under the right circumstances, but has not yet reached out to a broker to get a broker's opinion of value (BOV). If you notice an interesting property when you're driving through a submarket, you probably won't be able to identify the owner unless you subscribe to a real estate data service. But all the brokers in the market will know the detailed history of every multifamily property—who developed it, who represented it in the past, who owns it now, and who manages it. If it's not already listed for sale, you can reach out to your broker network and see if one of them might have a strong relationship with the owner, because they might know whether the owner would entertain an offer.

You can also find off-market properties through property managers once you have established relationships. We have very close relationships with our third-party property managers because they know our properties better than we do. The large management companies work with more than one set of owners, and they network among themselves. They can give you "insider" tips when an owner is thinking of selling, or connect you with the broker on a deal. They can also give you the best information on the pros and cons of a property's day-to-day operations.

I recommend buying off-market properties when you can. Negotiating for an off-market property is easier than competing against a large number of bidders, and you can usually get a better price. The more buyers who are bidding on a property, the less likely you will be able to get it at a price that makes sense for your business model. Sometimes a broker will approach us because the seller has a target price and wants a quick sale. They'll just ask if we can hit the number. We'll sign a confidentiality agreement and review the deal financials. Because we do so much background research on the submarket, it may not take long to figure out if we can make the deal profitable. We'll usually open with an offer less than the asking price, but the negotiation is quick and easy. Our fastest off-market deal took 3 hours to put under contract. The network you build can bring you deals that are never seen by the public.

With a fully-marketed deal, you might tour it twice, have 20 different versions of your underwriting, craft multiple bids with many hours spent on each one, and fill out a ton of paperwork. Then if someone outbids you, all that work was for nothing—that's the way it goes. With an off-market deal, you might only need a couple of versions of the underwriting and 2 rounds of bids before you get a "yes" or "no." That's much more desirable. Buying off-market can save a lot of repetitive work and increase your chances of winning the deal.

You'll rarely make a multifamily deal directly with the seller. It may happen occasionally with smaller properties in tertiary markets, but I've never actually seen one. If you're looking to invest in that type of market, you may be able to find an owner's information on a free site like LoopNet and contact them directly. We do have relationships with other operating groups, and it's not unheard of for an owner to make a private deal with a seller they already know. However, even in those situations, the seller will most often work with a broker to manage the transaction. For one thing, it makes the transaction more efficient and less stressful to have an experienced broker facilitating all the moving parts. For another, it's good business practice to maintain those broker relationships. When an owner had a great experience working with a broker when they bought the property, they'll turn around and make sure the same broker helps to sell it so they get the commission again. That kind of long-game mentality will build your reputation and build loyalty over time.

Think Long-Term

Even if you put in a ton of time and effort and wind up losing a deal, you can't burn bridges. It's frustrating to hear that a seller awarded the deal to someone else, but don't take that frustration out on the broker. I've heard groups get upset, swear they won't do business with someone again, or even cuss people out. That's so foolish and shortsighted! Frustrated or not, I'm still going to want to buy another property from them in the future. I always tell brokers, "I know it's tough on you, and you hate making these calls. We appreciate you letting us know. We'll see you on the next one. We appreciate all that you have done to help us on this one."

The longer you're in this business, the smaller the world gets. You're likely to work with the same brokers and the same sellers many times. If you have always been professional, courteous, timely, considerate, and a good communicator, you'll get pushed to the top of the list in a tight bidding situation. Brokers who enjoyed working with you in the past might advise a seller to approach you before listing a property to the public. A good reputation can be more powerful than deep pockets at finding and winning deals.

Hunting for great deals takes a lot of time and research. Investing the same time and care in your business relationships pays off exponentially because great deals start coming to you. Focus on building your reputation, following through on what you say you're going to do, and cultivating warm human connections with everyone in your network. After all, when someone has a deal in their pocket, are they going to want to work with a huge jerk who made their lives miserable, or a consummate professional who makes the transaction easy and treats them with respect and consideration? We're very careful with our business relationships (in addition to having a great team), and as a result we've been able to scale our operations faster than any other contemporary group.

Focus on the Numbers

Looking for a great deal is one thing. How do you know when you've found it? In order to determine whether a specific MSA and an individual property meet your investment criteria, you need to gather data and analyze it. In the next chapter, you'll learn where and how to gather the information you need, and how to determine whether a property will be a successful investment for your group.

Chapter 6

Analyzing Markets and Assets

Brandon Abbot and Danny Randazzo

The definition of a perfect investment property is crystal clear: it's a property that's going to generate cash flow and have an opportunity for significant capital appreciation. The only way to determine that is to go through a process of detailed underwriting analysis. If all the economic indicators of the market are good, and the financials of the property are good, then you can achieve your business plan.

You could find a property that looks good on paper. It's making a profit. But does it have year-over-year growth? As real estate investors, we want to see an asset's revenue grow year-over-year. If the fundamental economic indicators you relied on turn out to be inaccurate, the property could decline in value instead. Then your business plan will fail, and your investors won't receive the returns you initially projected for them.

For example, your plan might hinge on raising rents from, say, $1,300 to $1,500 per month. If you didn't do your market analysis and underwriting correctly, that rent increase could cause you to lose residents. With occupancy down, you won't make enough income—so not only are you missing the mark on your rent increase, your revenue is down overall. Your NOI winds up lower than when you bought the property.

Don't be swayed by a beautiful new complex. Do your research, because if the developers built it in a bad part of town with high crime, poor access, and no neighborhood amenities, people will move out. You'll be forced to lower your rent to stay competitive, which means you'll have a harder and harder time running your business. Pretty soon, your whole business plan falls apart, and the complex winds up dilapidated just like the other properties in the area.

A solid, achievable business plan must be based on facts and analysis, not conjecture or wishful thinking. In this chapter, you'll learn how to gather those facts and apply them. First, Brandon will walk you through analyzing a market. Then Danny will show you how to analyze a property and create a business plan for it, also known as underwriting.

Market Analysis

Recently we were looking at a very nice property in Charlotte, North Carolina. On paper it met all of our criteria: Charlotte is one of our submarkets. It was a brand-new Class-A community, built in 2020. It was **prestabilized**, meaning that it hadn't achieved 90% occupancy for 3 months, but since it was so new, people were still moving in, so that wasn't a red flag. It checked all the boxes at first glance.

However, we know that cities can be fickle. We knew a lot about Charlotte, but we didn't know every single neighborhood. We were just starting to do our research into the economic and social indicators of the area when we discovered that there was a 9:00 p.m. curfew. The crime was so bad that the police had the whole neighborhood locked down at night.

Would that asset ever attract enough Class-A residents to become stabilized? And if so, how long would it take, and how much trouble would there be along the way? It wasn't a bet I wanted to take.

You know the adage that the 3 most important factors in real estate are location, location, and location. It's true for multifamily communities as well—a fantastic property in a less than stellar location just isn't going to deliver on its potential. Thorough market research can guide you toward assets that will give you the best performance with the least risk and hassle. Evaluating fundamental economic indicators is paramount to making sound investment decisions.

Fundamental Economic Indicators

The traits you want to look for when you're searching for investment property are indicators that the economy is strong and developing in a way that drives a growing demand for apartments—and in our case, a demand for Class-A apartments, which are the most expensive. In an urban downtown area, Class-A rents could be anywhere from $4,000 to $8,000 or more per month at the time of writing. Then you have suburban Class-As, which would average $1,500 to $2,000 per month at the time of writing. The classes will have a slightly different slant in particular submarkets, but Class A is the top of the market. Remember, your goal is to increase the NOI from the property. You need to know if that's a realistic goal for this property in this area, in this town.

INCOME

First, we look at **median income**—the most commonly occurring income level. We also look for population growth. What type of businesses are active in the area, and is that industry thriving or declining?

There's an important difference between **average income** and **median income**. Average income adds the highs and lows together and finds the mathematical middle. That's not helpful for analyzing the potential demand for apartments because the mathematical middle doesn't tell you how the income is distributed. You could have a lot of low earners who can't afford your rent, and a few extremely high earners who aren't looking for apartments. The median income tells you what *most people* in the area are making. That's useful.

We want to look for the areas that have the highest median income. Those are the nicest parts of town. You want to see a median income of three times your target rental rate so you know that most people in the area can afford the rent you want to charge. Most people prefer to live within a reasonable radius of their job, their church, or their extended family—they have personal reasons why they live on one side of town or another. If the median income within a 3 to 5 mile radius of a property meets that three-times-rent threshold, then the neighborhood can support your rent goals.

POPULATION

Next, we look at the population—is it growing? More specifically, which parts of town are growing fastest? Where are new retail stores being built? What's the forecast for new businesses coming to town? What industries are driving the city's economy overall, and what are the prospects for those industries over the next 5 to 10 years? Look for announcements from major businesses, like Tesla announcing they're moving their plant to Austin, or Apple moving to Raleigh-Durham. Those employees are your future residents.

We like to see new major retail stores going into an area—Starbucks, Whole Foods, maybe a large regional chain like Publix. They do extensive market research before they undertake new locations, so you can piggyback off their research a bit.

When population growth is stagnant or the population is declining, you won't be able to push up your rents because demand is low. Just like anything else, rents obey the laws of supply and demand.

APARTMENT SUPPLY

That said, let's look at the supply side. While you're looking for signs of growth and new businesses, be on the lookout for new apartment construction as well. Those new complexes will be your competition.

If you buy a property that was built in 2005 and plan to upgrade it and raise rent, what will it do to your plans if a brand-new shiny community is going up right around the corner? They will likely offer discounts and incentives to help get the place leased up—two months' free rent on an eighteen month lease is a common example. With an empty complex to fill, that's going to affect the whole market for a while. You can't be as competitive because your property, however nicely you renovate it, is older. And you can't offer the same level of concessions because your property is full. Eventually that supply will be absorbed and the market will level out, but it will soften the results you're able to achieve with your property.

On the other hand, if the new complex winds up charging more rent once they're full, you can come in behind them and "draft" off of their higher rents by being the second or third most expensive in the market. Whether that new complex is a negative or a positive largely depends on timing.

Geography affects supply and competition as well. At one of our properties in Florida, we were happy to see that it has a nature preserve on one side, a residential neighborhood on the other, another apartment community on the third side, and a highway on the fourth. There was no way a developer could come in with a new complex right on top of us and soften our rents.

COST OF HOUSING

We also want to look at the cost of housing. If mortgage costs are very close to your target rents, that's a problem. The American dream is to own a home, and people are heavily indoctrinated that owning is always better than renting. If home values are hovering around $175,000 and you're looking to charge $1,500 in rent, then your potential residents could buy a house for a lower mortgage payment than they could rent from you.

The advantage of Class A multifamily properties is that folks with higher than average incomes are more likely to choose luxury apartment living for the ease and convenience. They don't want to mow grass or deal with replacing the water heater. They just want to call someone to have everything taken care of. If they were going to buy a house, it would be a much higher-end house. So by investing in areas with very high housing costs, you have more leeway to justify a rent increase without going over the cost of housing.

To get even more granular, we want to see the **average gross rental rate**—what other properties in the area are charging for rent, on average. The gross rental rate is calculated by adding up all the available rental units of different sizes and averaging by the total number of units. For example, let's say one-bedrooms rent for $1,000, and you have 15 of them available. Three-bedrooms go for $1,700 and you only have 3 of them available. Your average gross rental rate is $1,117. However, the distribution of apartment sizes weights your average. So if instead, you had 10 of the one-bedroom units and 8 of the three-bedrooms, your average gross rental rate would be $1,311. Comparing average gross rental rates for comparable properties and across the market gives you important information about the demand for larger or smaller apartments.

If comparable properties to yours are charging less than your target rent, pushing rents up to your target could be risky. You don't want to be the most expensive property in your submarket. You also need to make sure your comparables are actually comparable. If a community close by is charging $2,000 a month, and they have marble countertops, heated floors, and an on-site masseuse, then you aren't going to be able to charge the same with Formica counters, wall-to-wall carpet, in a community where you need pepper spray after 9 p.m. Making sure your goals are aligned with the market is crucial to achieving your business plan.

CASE STUDY: HOUSTON

When selecting a market, you're going to start big-picture and drill further and further down. We're looking for primary MSAs, large metro areas in the Southeast, like Houston, Raleigh, Charlotte, Atlanta, or

Charleston. Houston is one of the top ten primary MSAs in the country. It's got strong population growth overall, and we've targeted it as a good investment opportunity. But there are good areas and bad areas in any city, so we want to zero in on some choice neighborhoods.

Census data indicates that some neighborhoods are growing faster than others. So we might look at Baytown, on the southeast side of the city. It's along the coast near a lot of the oil-production industry. So there are plenty of employment opportunities, that's good. On the other hand, when we look at the median income of Baytown, it's a very blue-collar area. We're less likely to find a suitable property there.

The conditions are more favorable outside the number eight beltway. On the west side, you have the Katy area, and on the northeast side there's Humble. Both of those show median incomes that would support the rent ranges we'd want to charge.

So the next step is to get information from local people. We called up some of our investors who live in Houston and asked what they think of these parts of town.

After that, we traveled to Houston ourselves. We drove around different neighborhoods to see if they looked run down or thriving. Is it the older part of town, or is there a lot of new development? Look at practical issues that your residents will face. How accessible is the neighborhood? Is it close to the highway? If they work downtown or at one of the large new employers, how long will it take them to commute? Seeing the location in person helps us drill down into the nature of the market and determine whether it's a place people want to live, or a place where people *used* to want to live. That's important to the potential growth of your business.

CASE STUDY: COLUMBIA

By contrast, let's look at Columbia, South Carolina. Dan and I both live here. For one thing, it isn't a primary market. That's one of our basic criteria.

Next, we don't have many blue-chip businesses or new businesses coming in. They're all going to Greenville, where you'll find BMW, Michelin, and other well-established large employers.

In terms of demographics and population growth, there's a high military presence. That means people move in and out but don't stay long. Folks come through for basic training and then get transferred. If a new political administration comes in, they could change high-level policies at any time and reduce the number of personnel on short notice. This affects your population directly.

The University of South Carolina is there also, so there's a large student population. They tend to be transient too. The apartments tend to be used a bit heavier by university students and that may increase repair costs.

One really useful guide to positive and negative indicators is to learn what makes a property or a city attractive or unattractive to lenders and institutional investors. Banks and investors hesitate to enter areas with high military or student presence, for example. There's the cyclical nature of the population, and there tend to be issues with high wear-and-tear.

The average vacancy rate here is relatively high, which shows that demand for apartments isn't very strong. Without major new employers coming in, it's not likely to increase in the near future. That would make it harder to raise rents on a multifamily complex, no matter how nicely we upgraded.

All in all, much as we love this city for other reasons, our investing criteria knock it out of the running. It's a great place to live, but the economic indicators are too negative for multifamily investing.

Resources for Your Research

Thorough market analysis requires a lot of detailed information. Fortunately, there's a wealth of resources available for you.

CoStar (costar.com) is one of the largest commercial providers of information and analytics. It has all the data you might need for any city or property you're investigating. It compiles median income, median housing, population growth, vacancy rates, and pretty much any market data you could want. It can be a very expensive piece of software, depending on how many people you have on your team and how many licenses you need. We use it because it has everything we need in one place. Other commercial data providers include Axiometrics and Rentometer.

City-Data (city-data.com) is a free website that lists census data for any city in the US. It will show population change, median income, median gross rent, median housing costs, crime rates, and your other major economic indicators. You can also drill down by zip code and see detailed information like the percentage of renters versus homeowners, local business profiles, age, education level, and all kinds of demographic data. This resource will give you pretty much everything you want to know about a target city.

You can also find information about rents and apartment sizes in your target area on listing sites like Apartments.com and Craigslist.com. If you can't physically go out and tour comparable properties in your target area, you can put on your apartment-shopper hat and view properties on listing sites, as well as get basic information about average rents for different size units in the market.

The most important free resource you can tap into is relationships with local brokers. The best time to tap your broker network in a submarket is when they don't have anything listed there. If they have something they're trying to sell you, it's hard to get an objective opinion. That's why building your network of professional contacts is so important—so that you aren't just talking to your brokers about a particular deal they're working on. You can also call them up and ask their honest opinion of a different part of town or a property that they aren't handling.

When you've narrowed down a target area or a certain property, nothing beats boots on the ground—actually driving through the submarket. Visit at different times of day and night to see what life is really like there. Does it feel comfortable or sketchy? Your intuition or gut feelings about a property can give you amazing insights that you couldn't get any other way. Don't just rely on your own impressions. Ask the locals. If you get an Uber from the airport, ask your driver about the neighborhood or community you're visiting. When you tour a property, ask the postal carrier what kind of reputation it has. If locals are saying, "Oooh, it's rough," pay attention. If the prevailing attitude is, "It's beautiful, I'd love to live there someday," that's a great sign. Data can narrow down your search to a manageable number of places, but nothing can replace seeing a site with your own eyes.

Drill Down

When you've identified and analyzed your market, toured your submarket, and found a potential property, it's time to sharpen your pencil and make sure the numbers work. Danny, our finance guy, will introduce you to the art and science of underwriting.

Underwriting

Underwriting a deal is the process of evaluating the investment opportunity. You need to physically inspect the property and financially evaluate the asset to determine the potential return on investment it could provide. Underwriting is the mathematical evaluation of returns based on your financial analysis of the apartment community.

As an operator or active investor, you'll need to take an active role in underwriting, doing the legwork of property tours and research, and understanding how the financials and market fundamentals interact with each other. If you're a passive investor, you could probably skip this whole chapter, as long as you properly vet the operator of the opportunity you're planning to invest in, and have confidence that they can achieve their business model.

Work Backward

I'm sure you've heard the saying "Begin with the end in mind." You should take the same approach to underwriting a multifamily deal. Your end goal is to make money, so you work backward from there.

The first step is to set your return criteria: what return do you want to see on this investment? You might evaluate that goal as a cash-on-cash return, an annualized return, or an **internal rate of return**, but no matter which metric you use to express your goal, you need to have that end in mind.

Internal rate of return (IRR) is a performance measure for the return on an investment that takes into account the length of time it takes to see a return. A quicker return is more valuable than a slower return and therefore has a higher IRR. The IRR is most commonly used in multifamily real estate investing because it expresses a more comprehensive value to the investor than a simple metric like **return on investment** (ROI). ROI can be misleading because it doesn't factor in the length of the holding period on an investment. The complex equation of IRR accounts for the opportunity cost of having money tied up in an investment rather than liquid, and expresses that time is, in fact, money. You can find an in-depth discussion of IRR and ROI in the Knowledge Base at PassiveInvesting.com.

The more clearly you set and express your return criteria, the more quickly and reliably you'll be able to qualify or disqualify potential projects. As soon as it's clear that a deal can't accomplish your goals, you can stop wasting time on it and move on to a new opportunity. Working backward helps you get ahead faster.

Art and Science

Evaluating the financial performance of specific assets is both an art and a science. Underwriting from an artistic approach means you need to think creatively about the amenities and offerings that can attract and retain residents. In a way, you're thinking like a marketer or a product designer, to understand which features will appeal to your customers so you can build them into your product.

For example, if your property were in an area where no one kept dogs as pets (as unlikely as that may be), then it wouldn't be a good business decision to install a dog park. No one would use it, so they wouldn't pay a premium to live there. On the other hand, if every resident in your community were an avid swimmer, installing a pool or upgrading the pool would yield a higher premium because that amenity is valuable to your residents. You have to think about each deal differently and understand the localized economic indicators as well as the demographics of the region in order to ensure you can achieve your business plan.

From a science perspective, underwriting is pure math. The process is the same for every property: you take the number of units, the rental rate per unit, other income and fees, operating expenses, and determine the purchase price and capital improvements that will allow you to make the return you're seeking.

Financial Reports

When you're looking to buy a single-family home, you might estimate the utility costs by calling the gas or electric company to find out what sort of carrying costs the property might have. With multifamily deals, we get all the information about the property's income and expenses detailed in 2 reports: the **rent roll** and the **T-12**. You'll recall these are the same 2 reports Dan discussed in Chapter 4, that we release to our passive investors for the properties they're invested in.

These financials are provided by the brokers to anyone interested in making an offer on the property. All the income and expense, and profit and loss information about the property are in these 2 financial reports.

The rent roll is exactly what it sounds like: a list of the renters. It lists all the different floor plans, the total gross potential rent, and the total being collected. It shows how many units are leased and to whom. For each resident, it details how much the unit is leased for, whether the resident is paying any additional fees like pet rent, and whether they are behind or in collections. The T-12 report shows the gross potential rent and the total collected. It also details all the property's expenses, like payroll, utilities, and landscaping. The T-12 will also show your other income items. In addition to rent, you have utility bill-backs where the tenant pays their share of the water or gas and electricity. If you charge the residents for exterminator fees and other services, those will also show up.

A good property management group will provide you with a **proforma of operations**. This spells out the manager's projections of how much income they think the property could generate, how much they believe they could rent each unit for, and their estimate of expenses for managing the property. This type of report is a great tool to compare with your own underwriting, to see how close your estimates are. Pay close attention to any significant differences, and have a conversation with the property manager to figure out why you're projecting such different numbers. This can help you uncover and correct any misconceptions or knowledge gaps you may have about the property or about the market (or reveal opportunities to significantly improve operations by changing property managers) and make your underwriting model as accurate as possible.

Metrics

When you're evaluating an underwriting model, some of the most critical metrics to look at are your project's overall IRR, your yearly cash-on-cash return, your average cash-on-cash return, your annualized return, and the equity required to purchase the property.

Yearly cash-on-cash (COC) return is the percentage return you project for each year of the holding period. **Average COC** is the average for the whole period. For example, if your year 1 COC is 5%, year 2 is 10%, and year 3 is 15%, then your average COC is 10%.

All of these metrics are related to investor returns, which makes them critical to evaluating the deal. After all, the whole purpose of buying the property is as an investment vehicle. If the project can't meet your goals for investor returns, you can disqualify it quickly. If your underwriting shows that the deal can meet or exceed your target investor returns, then that's a property you want to pursue so your investors can put their money into an asset with strong performance and achieve their investment goals.

A number of additional metrics are important to understand when you're underwriting a deal.

Consider the **turn cost**: the cost to clean and prepare a unit when a resident moves out, to prepare it for someone new. That might include touch-up paint, shampooing the carpet, and other maintenance costs.

If the property offers **concessions**, those will be detailed on the rent roll. A concession is a discount on rent offered to help raise occupancy on a new property. When a property offers concessions, it could achieve full physical occupancy, but it might not have full economic occupancy if the residents aren't paying market rents. The difference between the rental income you should be getting, and the amount you're actually collecting, is known as **loss-to-lease**. Full physical occupancy without full economic occupancy creates a high loss-to-lease ratio.

Gross potential rent is the number of units you have, multiplied by the rental rate per unit.

Other income includes fees for various services, like an application fee, move-in or move-out fees, garage parking or a storage unit, or any other nonrent items charged to the resident.

Loss-to-lease is when you rent a unit for less than the market rental rate.

Vacancy loss represents the revenue you are missing on vacant units. When you underwrite a deal, you need to know the average vacancy rate in the area and reflect that in your underwriting calculations. You should never overestimate occupancy (or underestimate vacancy loss) in your underwriting. If anything, you should be conservative in your projections. The art of underwriting comes up again here, because you have to decide what a conservative estimate of occupancy would be for this property.

If you have a model unit on the property, that would be a **nonrevenue** generating unit, so you need to account for that in your effective gross income number.

Accounts receivable (AR) represents the percentage of residents who can't pay on time or have difficulty paying on time. That may turn out to be a **bad debt**, or a decrease to your overall income, if it's unlikely that it will ever be paid back.

Expenses include payroll, contract services, repair and maintenance, turnover, utilities, administration, marketing, legal, insurance, management fees to your third-party management company, property taxes, replacement reserves, and then any additional localized taxes, fees, or licenses that you may need to run your property. Those are the key metrics for understanding and underwriting a deal.

You can find a sample underwriting sheet that shows the interactions between these metrics in the Knowledge Base at PassiveInvesting.com.

Methods

In the last chapter, Brandon talked about market analysis. I want to emphasize that understanding the market is essential for effective underwriting, because the local market dictates the assumptions you can make about the occupancy levels you can expect and what rent the market will bear. You need to determine market rents for all the different size units in your community—1, 2, or 3 bedrooms. If you select the wrong market rent to base your analysis on, it could break the deal. Understanding the financials of the local market is going to help you hone in and be successful at underwriting.

Touring comparable communities helps you see your competitors' buildings and units so you can understand how their rental rates and units compare to yours. The best thing to do is present yourself as a prospective resident, say whether you're looking for a 1, 2, or 3 bedroom unit, get the 5 or 10 minute spiel from the property manager and go tour a unit. This way you can get a feel for exactly how it compares to the asset you're evaluating.

By taking market data from your research and comparing it with your tours of the comps, you can put together a rent comp analysis spreadsheet. This great tool enables you to compare your closest competitors, the amenities they offer, and the pros and cons of each property. If your closest competitor is offering units exactly like yours for $1,000 a month, then you should charge a bit less. You want to make sure your expectations are conservative.

Rent comp spreadsheets and other useful models are available in the Knowledge Center at PassiveInvesting.com.

Underwriting goes well when you conservatively underwrite a deal. Let's say you assume the vacancy rate for a market is 10%, and when you calculate investor returns with that assumption, the returns look very strong. Later, as you dig deeper into the market, you might discover that the vacancy rate for the last 5 years and the projected vacancy rate for the next 5 years are closer to 7%. That means you're likely to have higher occupancy than you expected, which means you can collect more income on a monthly basis. That strengthens your returns, which is great news for you and your investors.

The wrong way to do underwriting would be to be aggressive or take the broker's word at face value for everything. Remember, this is the person trying to sell you the deal. They may say that you could easily push up rents by $200 a unit, so you underwrite the deal on the assumption that you'll be raising rent from $1,000 to $1,200 a month.

Then, when you do your detailed market study, you realize that the broker sold you a load of hogwash. The absolute top of the range in your market is $1,100 a month. Now you have to go back and update your underwriting with the new numbers. When you're looking at a community with 150 to 300 units, that $100 difference per unit, per month, adds up to a lot of money! That difference could kill the deal. So in order to be successful at underwriting, you need to take a conservative approach and do all your homework on the property and your market up front. You want to effectively qualify deals and buy properties that meet your requirements instead of buying something because you get excited or a broker sold you a pretty story.

We've created several videos to help you through the underwriting process. These videos will teach you how to be conservative at underwriting and the key steps to develop a conservative underwriting process. You can find them on our website at PassiveInvesting.com/Toolkit.

Time to Implement

You've done your research, selected the property you want to pursue, and created a realistic business plan to make this investment profitable. Now you need to put those plans into action. In order to purchase the property you want, you have to bring together investor money and lender money. So how do you secure a multifamily loan, structure the cash flow and equity shares, and present the deal to your investors? That's what Danny and Dan will cover in the next chapter, Money Matters.

Chapter 7

Debt, Equity, and Deal Structuring

Danny Randazzo and Dan Handford

Once you identify a property that you'd like to acquire, you need to get your financing together so you can get your loan approved and close the deal on time. You and your investors will bring some of the money to the table for closing, commonly called equity. The rest you'll borrow from a lender, commonly called debt.

Since the terms of your loan will affect the way you structure the rest of the deal, we'll address financing first. Danny will unpack the major concepts and terminology you'll need to understand in order to find the best financing for your deal. Then Dan will discuss how to structure a deal that's attractive to your investors and profitable for you.

Financing Your Multifamily Property

When it comes to financing multifamily real estate, there are hundreds of lenders and many different types of debt options that can meet the specific needs of your project. Choosing the right debt option is a matter of balancing the needs of your project and your business plan with the requirements of a specific lender.

There are some general requirements you can expect from any lender in the industry. Other requirements vary according to the type of lender and the individual lender's assessment of the project (and of you as the operator). In this section, I'll walk you through how to find the best lender, the key types of lenders you'll encounter, basic lender requirements, and how to understand the terms of a multifamily loan.

Using a Debt Broker Versus Going Direct

A debt broker (also called a financing broker or mortgage broker) is a third-party intermediary who specializes in matching commercial borrowers with suitable lenders. The broker can provide all the information you need about current interest rates, amortization, and lender requirements like loan-to-value and loan-to-cost ratios. An excellent debt broker can help ensure that you're getting debt quotes from each type of lender to find the best fit for your project. A debt broker will charge you a fee for their service, but it is a valuable service to ensure that your investment is getting the best possible debt solution.

A direct loan is one that you negotiate directly with a lender rather than going through a debt broker. In some instances, you may need to clarify whether a financial institution is a direct lender. Direct loans can save you fees, but you forgo the guidance and market knowledge that a good debt broker can give when you aren't sure what type of loan is best for your deal.

Key Multifamily Lenders

There are 4 main types of lenders you might work with on multifamily deals: agency lenders, private lenders, commercial mortgage-backed security loans, and local financing. Let's unpack the features of each type.

AGENCY LENDERS

The Federal Home Loan Mortgage Corporation, commonly known as "Freddie Mac," and the Federal National Mortgage Association, referred to as "Fannie Mae," are government-backed agencies that make real-estate loans through a bank or lender. The agency lenders typically offer lower interest rates than other lenders and require a lower **loan-to-value ratio (LTV)**. Agency loans usually have longer terms. Agency lenders can be flexible with fixed or floating interest rates, depending on the marketplace.

When you're in discussions with a lender, it's important to ask whether they are a direct lender for Fannie Mae or Freddie Mac. Sometimes when you're looking for loans, it might be unclear whether you're dealing with a broker or the lender itself. In the industry, *good* debt brokers and lenders will be very helpful in explaining the ins and outs of the process. If anything in your conversations isn't making sense, you should keep looking until someone can explain everything very clearly and transparently to you.

If you already know that an agency loan is your best option, there's usually no advantage to working with a broker (and paying extra fees to the broker) because you can get the same terms and pricing by working with a direct lender. Working with a high-quality lender that knows the ins and outs of agency loans and the current economic environment will be extremely beneficial and make sure you are getting the best options for your investment.

LTV is the ratio of the loan amount to the appraised value or purchase price of the property. A low LTV presents lower risk for the lender, and a higher LTV is a higher risk. LTV = Mortgage ÷ Value.

Typically, an agency loan would be most appropriate for an existing, cashflowing asset with strong historical occupancy and a longer investment holding period—5 to 7 years or more. If you're considering an agency loan, it's very important to match your business plan to the duration of the loan, because it can be difficult to exit an agency loan. Many agency loans require significant prepayment penalties which could be into the hundreds of thousands or even millions of dollars, depending on the deal size and interest rate environment.

BRIDGE LOANS AND PRIVATE LENDERS

I group bridge loans and private lenders together because they work very much the same way. They typically offer higher LTV or higher leverage, meaning more debt on an investment purchase. They typically have higher interest rates than agency loans, but they are usually shorter-term loans that offer you more flexibility to pay off the debt early. The typical LTV for a bridge or private loan is about 75%, with a term of 5 years or less.

Private and bridge lenders are a good fit for newly built properties without much historical operating information, properties that need significant capital expenditures (CapEx), or properties with a poor historical performance that you plan to turn around. Heavy CapEx properties are called value-add deals. If you improve performance in a short time frame of 12 to 36 months, you can refinance the bridge loan into a longer term loan with a lower interest rate. Private loans can be advantageous for certain investment opportunities based on your business plan and equity needs.

CMBS

Commercial Mortgage-Backed Security (CMBS) loans are originated by life insurance companies, pension funds, and other balance-sheet lenders. These types of lenders predominantly have low, attractive interest rates. At the same time, they have some of the most conservative LTV ratios, meaning that as a borrower, you will not be able to get as much debt with these lenders compared to a private or bridge lender. Their terms are fairly flexible to compete against long-term agencies or, if needed, short-term options as well. CMBS lenders can meet the needs of all sorts of investment properties.

LOCAL LENDERS

As a rule of thumb, if you are looking for a loan smaller than $2 million, your best option is to go to a local community bank or credit union, or a regional bank in the target area. Local lenders can give you the best interest rates and loan terms on those smaller loans. If your loan size is between $2 million and $5 million, your best option may be a private lender or to go through Freddie Mac or Fannie Mae's small balance loan programs. If your loan is larger than $5 million, you'll want to compare quotes from agencies, private lenders, and CMBS lenders.

Lender Requirements

Lenders require certain credentials from borrowers in order to qualify them for a loan, and there are some standard terms that you'll find in any multifamily loan agreement. Let's take a look at the typical lender requirements you may encounter.

GUARANTOR OR KEY PRINCIPAL

As we mentioned in earlier chapters, a guarantor (also known as a key principal or loan sponsor) guarantees a loan with their personal net worth and liquidity. Lenders require that the managing partners or key principals of the group have a personal or combined net worth equal to the loan amount, and sufficient liquidity to service the loan in case the project struggles financially. In order to combine their net worth to meet lender requirements, the managing partners must sign onto the loan personally. The general rule of thumb for liquidity is that the guarantor(s) must have 10% of the loan balance in cash or cash equivalents. For example, if your loan is for $1 million, the lender will want to see bank statements or stock brokerage accounts totalling $100,000 in liquid assets.

If you want to become an operator and don't have sufficient net worth or liquidity, you will need to establish a relationship with a guarantor in order to meet lender requirements. It's important for you to consider these requirements in advance, before you are in the throes of trying to arrange financing for a deal.

RECOURSE VERSUS NONRECOURSE LOANS

A recourse loan is one in which the operating group is personally responsible to ensure repayment of the loan to the lender—in the event of anything going wrong with the property in which the SPE holding the property can't make loan payments, the lender's recourse is to get the money from you personally as the operator and guarantor. They will take the property as collateral and come after your own assets, if needed, to ensure the entire debt is repaid to the lender. One important aspect of working with a local lender is that typically a local lender will only offer 100% recourse loans.

Agency, private, bridge, and CMBS lenders normally offer nonrecourse loans. A nonrecourse loan is secured by the property itself as collateral. If the loan goes into default, the lender's recourse will be to take back the property in foreclosure. They won't come after your personal assets.

However, all lenders will require "bad actor" or "bad boy" carve outs. That means that if the borrower or guarantor commits fraud or does anything to destroy the property value or cause the property to go into default, the no-recourse loan becomes a recourse loan, and the lender can come after you as the operator for repayment. These carve outs protect the lender and the investors from negligent or criminal acts by the operator or guarantor.

OTHER REQUIREMENTS

Lenders need to inspect the property and may apply various other requirements to a loan. These will vary by lender and from one deal to another. For example, agency lenders will require that a property be stabilized (90% occupancy for at least 3 months). If the property doesn't meet agency requirements, you will need to work with other types of lenders.

You will also face insurance requirements. These usually include property and general liability insurance, and may include business-income insurance and an umbrella policy.

Reading a Term Sheet

A **term sheet** is a document provided by the lender that summarizes the terms a lender is offering on the loan. It is not binding and may go through several drafts as you negotiate the loan. It's usually a few pages long and will include the name of the lender, the property, the location, the borrower and guarantor, the amount of the loan, the expenses that the borrower will be responsible for, its recourse or nonrecourse requirements, and all the specific features of the loan. Let's define some of the terminology you may encounter.

You can download a sample term sheet in our Apartment Syndication Toolkit at PassiveInvesting.com/Toolkit.

A **loan assumption** can occur if a seller is trying to sell a property that has existing debt. As a buyer, assuming the existing loan might be a good option to get the property at a lower purchase price. If the existing loan is not as competitive as the current prevailing interest rates, you might negotiate a discount on the price to offset that. When you are making a new loan on a property, the term sheet will specify whether or not that loan could be assumed by a new owner in the future.

The term sheet states the interest rate on the loan and any interest rate cap requirement if the rate is variable.

An interest rate cap is an important risk-management tool to help plan your financing over the life of the deal. Essentially, it's an insurance policy that limits the amount of interest you have to pay on your loan, no matter how high the market interest rate might go. Typically these interest rate cap policies are written to come into play after an increase of

200–300 basis points from the original floating rate. A lender will usually have an index such as the Secured Overnight Financing Rate (SOFR) or the London Interbank Offered Rate (LIBOR) to determine the base rate and then add a spread on top of that. The interest rate cap typically comes into play when the interest rate starts to creep up above the floor set by the lender. For example, if you secure a loan with a variable rate at SOFR + 2.5%, the all-in rate might be closer to 3.5%. The interest rate could go much higher. At the time of this writing, we're seeing rates up to 8%, which is similar to the rate hikes of 2008. A significant rate hike can blow all your underwriting assumptions, make your operation unsustainable, and cause you to eventually lose your property.

At PassiveInvesting.com, we always buy interest rate caps, so our variable rates might go up 400 basis points (4.0%). In the example of securing a 3.5% loan, that would allow the rate to float up to 7.5%, but we are not on the hook for the higher interest above our purchased cap, even if the listed rate goes higher. Knowing the rate cap on our variable interest allows us to forecast that scenario in our underwriting and make sure the deal will still work for us and deliver a return for our investors. We consider interest rate caps so important that we tell our passive investors it's a red flag if an operator doesn't buy one. (You can read more about the effect of interest rate caps from the investor's perspective in Chapter 12.)

Interest rates are specified and negotiated in terms of points and basis points. A **point** means one percentage point. A **basis point** is one one-hundredth of one point (0.01%, or 0.0001 of the total amount). To say it the other way around, 100 basis points equals 1 point or 1%. The **spread** is the difference between a benchmark interest rate and the rate a lender is charging. **Benchmark rates** are the published rates used by international banks or offered on financially-traded instruments like government bonds. For example, if a lender charges 300 basis points over the 10-year US Treasury, the spread is 3% over the interest rate paid by US 10-year Treasury bond. The 10-year Treasury, LIBOR and SOFR, are commonly-used benchmarks.

Earlier, we discussed the importance of LTV (loan-to-value ratio). The term sheet will state the maximum LTV that the lender will accept. It also specifies other limitations on the debt, including **minimum debt service coverage ratio** required at closing **(DSCR)**, and the **minimum debt yield** required at closing. The DSCR is the relationship between a borrower's operating income and their debt obligations—it measures your ability to make your loan payments with cash flow. Generally, lenders will accept lower ratios in a growing economy and demand higher ratios in a slow economy or a recession. Debt yield shows the property's NOI as a percentage of the total debt, so debt yield equals the NOI divided by the loan amount.

Next, you'll find the duration of the loan and the **amortization** schedule (how much of each payment goes to principal and interest, which may change over the life of the loan). If the payments will be interest-only for a period of time, that is stated as well.

A **prepayment penalty** is a required fee you must pay the lender if you pay off the loan balance earlier than the stated term. It could be a fixed percentage of the loan balance, or it could be calculated based on the difference between the loan rate and the current interest rate at the time of payoff. The term sheet and loan agreement will outline how the fee is calculated. Some loans may also include a **commitment fee** when you agree to the loan and an **exit fee** whenever you pay it off.

Subordinated debt is a secondary loan that would be repaid after the primary loan is paid off. Some lenders and some loans will not allow you to take on subordinated debt for the property. The term sheet will also detail the securitization of the loan and the requirements for escrow, site inspection, insurance, and any other special conditions. States differ in how they document a loan's securitization. Some states use a record mortgage, some use a first lien, and some use a deed of trust.

As an active investor, when you receive term sheets from lenders, it's important to read and understand every word that's written because this is the summary of everything you'll be agreeing to in your loan agreement. If you are new to multifamily investing, you should have your attorney review all the documents as well.

While you are exploring your financing options and negotiating terms with your chosen lender, you will also need to begin planning the structure of your deal. A strong deal structure will give your investors great incentives to back your project, as well as making all your hard work pay off.

Structuring Your Deal

When we talk about deal structuring, we're talking about setting up your deal for success from the very beginning—when you are trying to raise capital, all the way to the end when you are exiting an asset. You need to entice your investors to invest in this project by making sure they can earn a nice return, while also being conservative enough to ensure you will hit or exceed your projected returns. In addition, you also want to make enough money yourself. There's a fine balance between creating enough return for your investors while also carving out enough of a chunk for yourself as the operator that you're motivated to keep growing the business.

My philosophy—our philosophy at PassiveInvesting.com—is that you should think more about your investors than about yourself. At the end of the day, you can't do these deals without your investors. If you're only thinking about yourself and your own profits as the operator, you'll do well in the short term. In the long term, you'll hold back your business growth or simply go out of business.

If you take care of your investors, then it will be easier and easier to raise capital going forward because you'll have repeat investors and a growing network of referrals. When your investors truly get to share in the upside of your project, you're rewarding them for investing with you. Then they'll want to invest with you more and more, and encourage their family, friends, and colleagues to do the same.

The 3 main components of your deal structure are your fees and waterfall, including your capital stack structure. You need to make decisions in each area that will give you a good return on the time, energy, and effort you're putting into the project. At the same time, you need to offer your investors a solid return for trusting you with their money.

Fees

There are a few common fees that you can build into your deal. I discussed them briefly in Chapter 1, so I'll give some more detail and expand on how these fees affect your deal structure. Remember, the investors are buying shares in the SPE that you create to purchase the property. So any fee that's paid to the operator by the SPE is coming from the investors' money. Some operators try to make their projects look more attractive by touting the fact that they don't charge any fees, but they make up that money by taking more equity out of the capital stack. I don't recommend you do that. You deserve to get paid for your work, and your investors deserve to see where their money is going, and why.

ACQUISITION FEE

The acquisition fee is paid upon closing when you acquire the property. It can be based on the purchase price or on the total transaction costs. Total transaction costs would include the purchase price and any planned capital expenditures, along with closing costs. The acquisition fee is normally between 1% and 4%, depending on the size of the deal. The smaller the deal, the larger the percentage, and vice versa.

GUARANTOR FEE

The guarantor fee compensates the guarantor for maintaining the net worth and liquidity required by the lender, and standing good for the loan. The fee is normally between 1% and 3%, and may also be calculated on either the purchase price or the total transaction costs.

ASSET MANAGEMENT FEE

The asset management fee is a monthly fee paid to the operator for their work in overseeing the asset's financial and overall operational performance. In practical terms, that often means weekly phone calls with the property manager to monitor and manage performance, and visiting the property on a regular basis to check up on the on-site property manager. If necessary, it may mean replacing the property manager to improve performance. It also entails keeping the investors informed of performance through regular reports, distributing monthly cash flow to investors, making sure the annual tax documents are sent out on time, and so forth. The asset management fee is typically between 1% and 3%, and it can be calculated one of two ways.

The most common way to calculate the asset management fee is as a percentage of an asset's gross income in the prior month. This is the structure most commonly used in a single-property or deal-by-deal syndication. However, if your funding structure includes multiple assets in a single deal, then you'll usually see the asset management fee based on the overall amount of equity in the syndication.

CAPITAL EVENT FEE (DISPOSITION OR REFINANCE)

The capital event fee, disposition fee, or refinance fee are terms that can be used more or less interchangeably. A **capital event** is when there is a transaction or change in the asset's capital outside the normal course of business. So if you sell the asset (disposition) or refinance it, those are both capital events. The fee is normally between 1% and 3%. For a disposition, it's calculated on the sale price of the property. For a refinance, it's calculated on the total proceeds received from the refinance or supplemental loan.

There are a number of other fees operators might build into their deal structure, some of which we use, and some that we don't use. You can find the full rundown of potential fees in Chapter 1 under "How Operators Make Money."

The Cash Flow Waterfall

The revenue from your property will pay expenses and fees (including the asset management fee), debt service payments, and then the leftover cash flow will flow back to your investors in a structure known as a waterfall. If the property performs well, some of the cash flow may also come back to you as a performance incentive called a **promote**. Think of the waterfall structure as a bucket brigade.

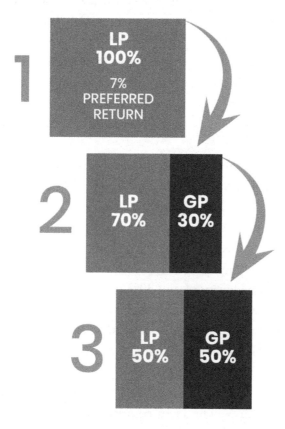

Imagine a series of buckets that descend like a staircase. Money is going to flow into the top bucket, overflow, and then spill into the next bucket down. When that bucket fills up, it will overflow and spill into the next one, and so on down the line. This represents how the profit from your property will be distributed to the investors and to you. We use waterfall models for both the monthly cash flow being distributed during the holding period, and for distributing income from a capital event like a refinance or sale.

The volume of each bucket—how much money it will hold before it overflows—is called a **hurdle**. For your monthly distribution of cash flow, imagine the cash flow generated from the property filling up the top bucket. This bucket represents a category called the **preferred return**, which goes to your investors first. One hundred percent of the cash flow from the property goes into this bucket until it hits the hurdle. A typical preferred-return hurdle for a multifamily deal would be 7% annually, but I have also seen it as low as 4%, or up to 12% (which is rare). So all the cash flow goes straight to the investors until they have received 7% on their investment, which is the first hurdle in this example.

When the income from the property exceeds 7% of the total investment, that bucket overflows into the second bucket. This second bucket represents an **equity split**. This money will be split between you, the operator, and the investors. Equity splits can be divided up any way you like. I've seen everything from 50/50 to 80/20 to 95/5. The most common equity split at this level for a multifamily deal is 70/30: that's 70% to the investors, and 30% to the operator. So this portion of the cash flow is split until the total amount of income reaches the next hurdle. This second hurdle is usually defined by the asset's IRR. A typical hurdle for this level might be a 13% IRR. That's the second hurdle in this example.

When the second hurdle is reached, that bucket overflows into the third bucket. This will be a new equity split that gives the operator a larger share than the earlier equity split. So, if the second bucket was a 70/30 split, the third bucket might be a 50/50 split. That means that if the operator succeeds in creating a return on the investment that exceeds a 13% IRR, they are rewarded with a greater share of the profits.

Now, there might not be enough money to fill up the second bucket. It might only fill halfway, so the equity split would stay at 70/30. If the operator doesn't deliver on the business plan, it's possible there might not even be enough money to fill the first bucket. The extra incentives for the operator only kick in after the investors receive their preferred return. Those equity splits are performance hurdles for the operator if they do a great job making the property profitable while executing on the business plan.

You can create as many buckets in your waterfall as you want, but of course it adds more and more complexity to the deal structure. You could even have a point—maybe 20% IRR—where the operator would receive the larger share of equity, like a 30/70 split, for really outperforming expectations.

We stop at 3 buckets in most of our deals. After the 2 hurdles of preferred return and the first equity split, we have all the excess go into that 50/50 split.

CATCH-UP PROVISIONS

Let's look at a different structure. This is a similar waterfall as the previous example, but with a catch-up provision for the operator on the preferred return. I actually discourage people from doing this, but you will see it used often, so you should understand it.

In this waterfall, you start out more or less the same: the top bucket represents the preferred return, with a hurdle of 7%. When the return exceeds the hurdle, it spills into the second bucket. However, in this version, the second bucket is referred to as the **operator catch up**.

The idea is that this bucket will catch the operator up to what they would have earned if there had been an equity split all along. So 100% of the cash in this bucket goes to the operator until they receive the equivalent of a 70/30 split on the first bucket. Once the catch-up bucket is full, the cash flows into a normal equity split of 70/30. There could be further hurdles and buckets added to this structure as well.

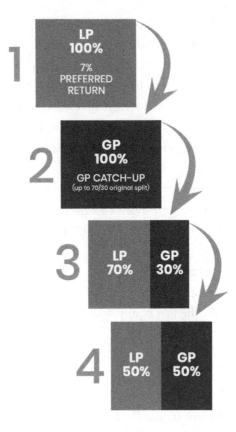

The issue I have with the operator catch-up structure is that it's very, very expensive for investors. It's nearly always going to be too expensive for the deal to make sense, unless the operator plans the deal to include a refinance. That's risky because you never know what kind of refinance terms you might get 3 to 5 years in the future. I never recommend that you underwrite a deal with a refinance built in. I certainly advise passive investors to stay away from deals with an operator catch-up provision.

For more information about waterfall structures, you can visit the Knowledge Center on our website at PassiveInvesting.com and search for "Waterfall."

Your Capital Stack

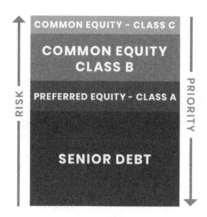

A **capital stack** refers to putting together the capital you need to close the deal to include both debt and equity. It shows the different sources of capital and the proportion that each will represent. Normally, your debt will represent 55–80% of the purchase price. The remaining 20–45%, plus CapEx, closing costs, and fees, would be part of the equity you raise from your investors (and your own coinvestment as the operator alongside the LPs).

Take a look at the illustration. The position of each item shows the order in which people get paid back when the property is refinanced or sold. The layers are paid from the bottom up, and each item must be fully paid before the next layer starts getting paid.

Now, just to be clear, many people build these capital stacks backward from the top-down. That makes no sense at all to me. How can you stack anything from the top down? You build a stack of things from the bottom up. I think of the layers of my stack as building Lego blocks. The first block goes on the table and you build up from there. Your capital stack is built in the very same way.

The priority in which capital sources are repaid is called **seniority**. In the first part of the chapter, Danny referred to subordinated debt. That's another way of referring to the layers of the capital stack—a

subordinate item has lower priority. Each layer from the bottom up is **senior** to the layers above it, and each layer from the top down is **subordinate** to the layers below it.

The largest piece of capital in buying a property will be the loan you take out—debt. So that goes on the bottom. The second position is equity—the money you receive from investors. Some deals have two layers of investor capital, **preferred equity** and **common equity**. Others only use common equity. Finally, operator equity goes on top.

Each layer in the stack has a different amount of risk and a different potential return based on the risk profile of the particular layer. The bottom of the stack (debt) has the lowest risk, and the operator (that's you) has the highest risk. If there isn't enough money from a refinance or sale to pay everyone in the stack, then the losses are greatest at the top. Risk and return always go together when you're investing, so the lender also receives the lowest return and the operator has the potential to receive the highest return.

When we look at the debt layer, the lender has the lowest risk because they structure the loan agreement in order to minimize or eliminate their risk. They have legal recourse against the guarantor in some cases, or the ability to foreclose on the property in order to ensure they get paid back. The loan agreement also sets a cap on the interest they will receive. Right now, interest rates for multifamily loans are hovering around 4% to 6%. You could also have senior debt (your primary loan) and **junior** or **mezzanine debt**, if there is more than one loan on the property. Junior or mezzanine debt could be used as part of the purchase price, or could be taken out later for capital improvements, as long as the senior lender allows it. The senior debt must be paid first. Up at the top of the stack, the operator has the highest risk and return. In the middle, the investors have the sweet spot of moderate risk and moderate return.

PREFERRED EQUITY

The equity portion of your capital stack can be divided differently for different classes of investors. Preferred equity is just above the debt layer. It has the lowest risk because it's paid back first, but returns are capped at a certain agreed upon level. We discussed preferred returns in the cash flow waterfall, and preferred equity works in a similar way. Preferred equity returns are typically between 8% and 12%. After the preferred equity is paid out, the remaining profits will be subject to an equity split—a 70/30 split is common, but it could be split in a variety of different ways.

Common equity doesn't start getting paid until the preferred equity is paid out, so the risk is slightly higher. However, the return on common equity is not typically capped. The profits may be split between Class A and Class B or Class C common equity, and if there is a great upside on selling the property, then those shares higher in the capital stack will collect more and more profit.

Bear in mind, there will only be equity to split if you increase the value of the property and sell it at a profit. As the operator, the equity split (also known as the **promote** we mentioned earlier) is a performance bonus you can earn, and the better you do at improving or realigning the property, the bigger bonus you'll receive.

COMMON EQUITY

Most of our projects don't use preferred equity, but we do use Class A and Class B common equity. Our equity as the operator is represented by Class B shares. With this structure, the debt is paid, then the investors get their initial investment returned, and then profits are split between the Class A and Class B shareholders. Again, this will be subject to an equity split. For example, 70% to Class A and 30% to Class B.

How does that translate to a better return for Class B? Look again at the illustration. The Class A layer is bigger. Those shareholders are putting a lot more money into the project. There are more people investing, or they are each making larger investments, or both. The Class B shares represent a smaller initial investment—mostly sweat equity. So when the profits are split 70/30, that 70% going to Class A is getting divvied up into a lot more pieces. Each dollar invested is getting a smaller portion of the pie. The 30% going to Class B is being split fewer ways, so each dollar of Class B is getting a better return.

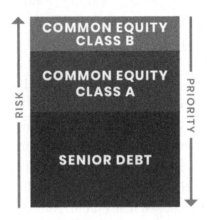

It's important for investors to understand where they fall in the stack, because they may want to be in a good position to minimize risk, or they may want to maximize their potential return even if it means higher risk.

Planning Your Equity Slices

We're frequently asked by investors, or other operators, to explain the reasons why we offer preferred equity on some deals and not others, or how we determine how much preferred equity to include. These decisions are based on the amount of cash flow from the property, and the analysis of different scenarios we run during underwriting. (We'll discuss the reasons an investor might choose to invest in common or preferred equity shares in Chapter 12.)

Preferred returns are paid out of your cash flow to holders of preferred equity shares. So whether you can include a preferred equity slice in your deal depends on how much cash flow you have to work with. Normally, preferred equity shareholders get a senior position in the capital stack, higher preferred returns, and no participation in the back end of the deal when you sell. Common equity shareholders get lower preferred returns from cash flow, but they get to participate in the back end appreciation of the asset when you sell. However, you still need to offer *some* cash flow to your common equity shareholders. Otherwise, you'll have a hard time raising money for the deal. Most passive investors prefer to receive cash flow during the holding period. Very few would be willing to wait for a sale to get their returns. We usually try to target between 6% and 9% cash-on-cash to the common equity shareholders during the holding period.

Back in Chapter 6, we discussed the underwriting process. During underwriting, you can experiment with different ratios in your capital stack to see whether preferred equity makes sense for your deal, and how much of your capital stack should be composed of preferred equity shares. You might start off with preferred equity as 30% of your capital stack, but if you determine that there wouldn't be enough cash flow to distribute to that many preferred investors, then you might reduce it to 10% or 15%, or eliminate it entirely. For example, in a recent deal in Myrtle Beach we offered only one common equity slice. The state of the debt market meant that our debt service ate up too much of our cash flow to offer preferred equity at all.

There are also different ways to split up your preferred returns, so if you offer 10% preferred return, you might pay 5% as cash flow during the holding period and the remaining 5% when you sell. You can modify your plans for the capital stack during underwriting, but in the end, it's really hard to do deals that include both preferred and common equity without a lot of cash flow.

Check out the Knowledge Center at PassiveInvesting.com for more information about understanding capital stacks.

Timing is Everything

Once you have identified a property that you'd like to make an offer on, you must be prepared to move quickly. A fully marketed property normally has a four-week marketing phase. The broker will send out information to their prospective buyers, schedule tours, and end the offering phase with a call for offers deadline.

That four-week time frame means that, depending on when you become aware of the deal, you will have between 1 and 3 weeks to get your underwriting done, your on-site tour, your pre-LOI physical inspection, and your capital stack finalized. For some deals, it could be even faster—we've had deals come across our desk on a Wednesday, tour the property on Thursday, and get under contract on a Friday.

This intense pace is yet another reason why it's just not feasible to become an operator as a side hustle, and why it's vital to have experienced, responsive members on your internal and auxiliary teams. In order to move this quickly on a deal, you must already understand the loan options available to you and be able to decide which one is appropriate for your deal. You must have existing relationships with investors, so you can get their commitment to a soft reserve and be confident in making an offer. You must thoroughly understand underwriting and how to structure a capital stack. You need to have systems and standard documents ready to plug in the information for a new deal. You have to know your business inside and out.

To help get you there, let's study the process of bidding, offers, and closing in detail. That's the topic of Chapter 8: Acquisitions.

You can find examples of fee disclosures, cash-flow structures, and capital stacks in our Apartment Syndication Toolkit at PassiveInvesting. com/Toolkit.

Chapter 8

Acquisitions

Brandon Abbott and Dan Handford

Back in Chapter 4, Dan mentioned the stress of raising capital for the very first property we bought. It was a 130-unit community in Greenville, South Carolina, and we bought it for $8.9 million.

We'd participated in other deals in the past with more experienced partners, but this was the first deal we did entirely on our own. We went through several rounds of bidding. With our business plan and financial projections, we decided that $8.9 million was as high as we could possibly go.

We lost the deal. The broker called and said, "Sorry, unfortunately there was one other group ahead of you. They offered $9.1 million, so the seller awarded the deal to them." Of course, we were bummed! We had been working hard on many different deals (as we still do), and it was very difficult to see all that time and energy spent with nothing in return. But that's the nature of this business, so we let it go and moved on.

Four weeks later, the broker called us back. The winning buyer couldn't finalize the negotiations. They never even got to the point of signing the contract. The seller was fed up and ready to give the deal to someone else. The broker asked if we were willing to renew our last offer.

Honestly, our first inclination was to apply some leverage. After all, they were coming back to us, and we knew they were stuck. We might have the opportunity to reduce our offer price or our earnest money, or otherwise give ourselves a little better terms. But instead of giving a quick answer, we asked the broker for a little time for the partners to talk among ourselves and double-check our numbers to make sure we were still good.

We called our mentor who helped us get started in the multifamily space. That call was exactly 1 minute and 47 seconds long.

He already knew about the deal, so we updated him on the current situation and asked what we should do. We were excited to have all the leverage on our side, and we were ready to use it. Our mentor said, "Don't do that. Accept the deal with your last offer. Make your life and your broker's life easy, because this won't be the only deal you get from him. But if you go back and forth with him on this one, he's not going to appreciate it, and you might not get deals from him in the future. Don't just think about the immediate win. Think long-term."

We did exactly that. We took the deal for $8.9 million and got the contract signed pretty quickly. That was an "Oh, crap!" moment. We'd put down $100,000 of nonrefundable earnest money on day 1, and we had to raise $2.5 million in capital in 60 days. Nowadays that doesn't sound like much because we regularly put $1 million down, but we also have a lot more experience and resources to back it up.

We all had butterflies in our stomachs. We made this enormous commitment, and now we had to do something about it. Raising the capital on that deal was the hardest part of the whole process, because our investors were really taking a chance on us. It took us the entire 60 days of the closing period, but we managed to close it on time.

Acquisition is the point at which all your relationship building, analysis, and planning becomes real. It's time to sign contracts and put down real money. Up to this point, we've discussed selecting your criteria and your market, how to identify a profitable investment property and make your business plan, and how to get the money together to buy it. We haven't talked much about the negotiation process or about competition. After all, if a property has excellent profit potential, you won't be the only group interested in it. You need to use the relationships and knowledge you've built in order to craft a winning bid. Then, after you put the property under contract, there are a lot of steps—and a lot of potential pitfalls—between contract and closing the deal.

In this chapter, Brandon will walk you through the stages of bidding on a property and strategies for successful negotiations. Then Dan will cover how to move from contract to closing.

The Bidding Process

As we discussed in Chapter 5, when a property goes on the market it will be represented by a broker who will serve as the intermediary in bringing bids to the owner. You want to cultivate good relationships with brokers to make sure they are sending you appropriate properties when they come on the market, and to build their confidence that you can close the deal.

Let's assume you've already built some high-quality broker relationships. Potential deals are flowing into your inbox. You find one that you like, make sure it matches your criteria, and you're ready to start underwriting to see if you should make an offer. Your first step is to contact the broker.

Pricing Guidance

The listing broker will generate a report for the seller as they prepare to list the property. They examine the property's financials, assess the general state of the market, and estimate the low, medium, and high ranges that they believe the property is likely to fetch. The broker will give potential buyers the medium price range of that estimate as guidance. This is a standard report called a **broker opinion of value (BOV)** or a **broker price opinion (BPO)**.

Call the listing broker and ask for their opinion pricing guidance. The broker might represent that price as an estimate per door, or as an overall total. For example, they might quote me $150,000 per door, or they might express the same price as $45 million. I know they are quoting the middle of the range because they hope (and expect) that the bidding will drive the price up.

The broker always wants to reach or exceed the high end of the pricing range, but they don't want to oversell their services to the owner. The low end of the range is the price they are very confident they can bring in. The middle and high end are the price they believe they could get if the bidding goes well. They never plan to sell the property for the low end of the range so they give their guidance based on the middle.

At the same time, you should request the property's financial reports (the T-12 and rent roll) and the property manager's proforma of operations. The broker will use these reports to give you a projection of how much you could raise the rent and how much it might cost to achieve that increase. You'll be required to sign a confidentiality agreement in order to receive this information.

Finally, you need to know the **call for offer** date **(CFO)**. This is the date offers will be due. This will normally fall 30 days after the property is listed. You need to know your time frame for figuring everything out. If for some reason, you're getting the information late and the CFO is only a week away, then you'll need to push. If the deadline is 3 weeks away, you may have other projects to attend to first.

Analysis

Your next move is to assess these reports to see whether you can underwrite a plan that would be profitable. In addition to the pricing guidance and broker offering memorandum or OM, you'll rely on your own analysis of the market and your own experiences from touring the property. How much capital expenditure will you need to budget for, and how much do you believe you could increase NOI?

As Danny mentioned in Chapter 6, you can't put all your stock in the broker's projections. They may tell you that the rent is trailing the market by $150 per door, so you can certainly raise rents by that much if you renovate. Keep in mind that these estimates aren't always realistic. They're trying to sell you a property. They're going to talk it up. It's useful to see what properties they use as comparables to see how close their projections might be.

If the listed property is a garden community built in 1995 with rents at $1,100, and the comparable property is a mid-rise complex built in 2020 with a parking garage that's achieving $1,500, it's not realistic that you would be able to raise rent by $400 per door, no matter how much you renovate. Residents who would go to the 2020 property aren't going to consider the 1995 community. There will be a great deal of useful—and factual—information in that broker OM, but don't take anything at face value.

You should also look at your ability to cut expenses. How many staff members are on the property right now and in what roles? Does the property really need 3 leasing agents or would 2 be enough? How about the maintenance crew? If you already own a property in the neighborhood, could you share staff between them? We'll look further into property management and adding value in Chapter 9, but these are the sorts of questions you should ask.

Make sure you check the property tax and insurance rates. You will be buying the property for more than the owner paid, which means those assessments will increase. How frequently does the property get reassessed, and when will those increased costs kick in?

While we underwrite a property, we stay in communication with the property manager and our asset manager. Before we move to the next step of the deal, it's important to make sure everyone is in agreement about how realistic these assessments are. We ask the property manager questions about changes we're considering—for example, could they run the property effectively with only 2 leasing agents, or is the current staff level necessary? You never want to set someone up for failure, so we want to make sure everyone agrees with our underwriting assumptions.

Use the broker as a resource to answer your questions. That might include details about financial items like taxes and insurance or questions about the residents and the neighborhood. The act of having multiple conversations is just as important as the information you get out of them. If you just get the financials and disappear until offers are due, they'll think you were never seriously interested. They may lean toward another group that stayed in contact and closely collaborated with them in the process. The broker needs to know that you are interested and actively working on your underwriting so they can expect a competitive offer from you.

Set Your Strike Price

Based on the broker's guidance and your own underwriting, you'll calculate your strike price. This is your outside limit—the highest price you can afford to offer that will still make the deal profitable.

Plan for that price to be higher than the broker's guidance, because you know the owner will want to get more than the middle of the range if they can. The agent also wants to get the highest price they can, because their commission is based on the sale price. Their interests are aligned with the owner to sell the property at as high a price as possible.

If your initial offer meets the price guidance, that's good. But when the second round of offers comes in, if you're still in the middle of the range, you'll get beaten out of the deal. Make your initial offer good enough to get noticed but leave yourself room to keep bidding before you hit your strike price.

Make Your Offer

When the CFO date arrives, you'll present your offer in the form of a **letter of intent (LOI)**. The LOI is a nonbinding agreement that states the amount of your offer, how much earnest money you can put down, and how quickly you are prepared to close. Normally LOIs are sent by email.

You can see an example Letter of Intent in our Apartment Syndication Toolkit at PassiveInvesting.com/Toolkit.

Since you already went to all the trouble of building a good rapport with the broker and have been talking to them regularly throughout the process, you can tap into that resource on offer day. Call them up and ask where the other offers are coming in. Are other groups offering close to the pricing guidance? It's always possible that the broker was overly aggressive on their BOV, and offers are coming in lower than they expected. If you just work off the guidance number and don't follow up, you could overprice yourself in the initial round. Stay in touch with the broker and ask what price will get your bid into the best and final offer round.

The **best and final** round is a short list of the top bids from the strongest contenders. If 30 to 50 different operating groups make initial offers, the top 5 to 10 will make it into the best and final. That decision is based not just on pricing, but also on which groups the broker believes are the most viable and the most likely to see the transaction through successfully. That's where your rapport with the broker makes a significant difference. If they know you, know your track record and that you are easy to work with, you'll have the advantage. Even if your pricing lags a little bit, your credibility can put you over an unknown group offering more money. You want to aim for the sweet spot of the lowest bid that will still make the cut because you haven't even started negotiating yet. The initial bid is just pulling the cord on the engine. The best and final is when things really start to move.

As a new operator, you won't have a track record of successful deals to support you (yet). You should certainly do what you can to build your broker relationships ahead of time. You can make your initial offer more competitive by optimizing your offer price, your earnest money, and your time to closing.

Sharpen Your Pencil

Once you are in the best and final round, the real negotiation starts. You need to look at your underwriting from different angles, to see how changing your assumptions could change the terms you can offer to beat out the competition.

Go back to your property manager and asset manager to see where there might be wiggle room. Are they confident about your potential rent increase, or is there anything you could do to push it even higher? Could you add amenities to make the property more competitive? Are there any savings or items that could be cut out of your CapEx budget?

On the financial side, what could you change to improve your returns? Perhaps you could increase the holding period of the property. Perhaps you could increase the number of Class A shares and alter the capital stack to change the equity distribution. You're pulling all the levers available to see how it alters the profitability equation, which in turn gives you the ability to offer the seller a higher price.

Similarly, if you set your strike price based on underwriting for 92% occupancy, could you raise it? Well, if the submarket is yielding 96% occupancy overall, then a conservative number would be 94%. You found a lever.

If you underwrite for 97% and make a very high offer on that basis, your business plan isn't going to be achievable. On the other hand, you could also lose out by being too conservative. If the market is yielding 96%, but you keep your underwriting at 90% to stay on the safe side, that's going to constrain how much you can offer. You're not going to win the deal because other groups with a more realistic model will outbid you.

While you're entertaining all these "what-if" scenarios, it's important to stay grounded in the economic fundamentals of the market and keep your projections conservative. Winning the deal isn't a "win" in the long run if you can't execute your business plan. If you overassume your potential rent increase, for example, you won't be able to deliver on it in real life. Failing to increase the rent sufficiently will mean you can't give your investors the money they're expecting. Make sure your underwriting assumptions are achievable, and check them with people who are active in the local submarket. Stay conservative but realistic in your underwriting assumptions.

The Psychology of Bidding

The best and final round is the prime time to tour the property. Of course, if you're in the area earlier, it can be convenient to bundle several tours together. But as a general rule it doesn't make sense to tour every property at the initial offer stage—you'd waste thousands of dollars in airline tickets, and you'd never be home. Touring at this stage also shows interest and competence. The seller is less likely to take your offer seriously if they know you've never even set foot on the property—it looks like you don't know what you're doing, or at least gives the impression that you are not paying attention.

Better yet, have the managing partners tour the property instead of relying solely on your acquisitions team. From time to time, we'll arrange a tour like this as a show of force. We'll charter a jet, hire a car from the airport, and make sure the broker knows about our travel arrangements. It underscores that we're committed to the deal and have the financial backing to close it.

Once you determine what you *could* offer, you need to decide what you *should* offer. During the best and final round, stay in close contact with the broker. Find out as much as you can about the seller's circumstances and priorities. Are they a big corporation, a wealthy family, or an individual? What is the seller most interested in—the highest price or the quickest closing? Use these insights to make your best and final offer as compelling as possible.

If you're a new operator and you're bidding against a group the broker has worked with before (like PassiveInvesting.com), offering the highest price won't necessarily get you the deal. The broker will favor the group they've worked with before because they have confidence in their ability to raise the capital, secure the loan, and close on time. They also know whether that group is easy to work with and will reduce their headaches in getting the deal done. If your bid is higher, the broker will go to the more established operator and say, "If you can meet this price, the deal is yours."

Instead of relying on price, sweeten your offer with other features that the seller wants. If they are under pressure to exit by a certain date because of their capital structure, or for any other reason, then you can make a special effort to close early. Normally it takes 30 days to do due diligence before closing, and then 30 days for the bank to approve the loan. If you can cut the due diligence period down to 20 days, then you can close in 50 days instead of 60. There are no secrets to closing quickly—you can't afford to skip steps. You just have to get all the steps done faster. It's pure hustle. This is where your full-time focus, your extensive preparation, and your responsive ancillary team members can really shine.

EARNEST MONEY

You have another powerful negotiating point in the way you structure your earnest money. In general, there are 2 **earnest money deposits (EMDs)** on a multifamily deal. The initial EMD is made when your bid is accepted and you put the property under contract. A typical EMD would be 1% of the purchase price, and it's standard for the initial EMD to be **soft money**. A soft money deposit is fully refundable if you decide to walk away from the deal. **Hard money** is nonrefundable.

During the due diligence period, the initial EMD remains in escrow, and it's contingent on your full inspection of the property, the lease audits, the legal verification of the property's title and boundaries, and so forth. If anything turns up during due diligence that would make the deal less attractive or changes the underwriting parameters, you might decide that your business plan isn't viable after all. For example, if you discover that the roof needs to be replaced or the parking lot needs to be resurfaced, you might not have accounted for that in your capital expenditure planning. If the seller isn't open to adjusting the price, a soft money deposit would let you walk away and get your money back.

When your due diligence is complete, the initial soft money EMD goes hard and becomes nonrefundable. At the same time, there will be a second EMD due, which is normally an additional 1%, for a total of 2%. The second EMD is hard money on day 1.

If you need a leverage point to strengthen your bid, you could offer hard money for the initial EMD. It's a strong move. You're putting your money where your mouth is. You'd need a high degree of confidence that you definitely want to buy this property. That needs to be based on doing your homework thoroughly, and you need to be in a financial position to have a high risk tolerance. It's a negotiating tactic that works very, very well. You should reach out again to the broker to ask whether anyone else is putting hard money down. Not many groups are willing to do that, so if the deal is right, it can be a good way to set yourself apart. This is usually only contingent on the legal status of the property—that the boundaries are represented correctly (survey), there are no issues with the owner's title to the property (title), and the ground isn't contaminated (phase one). If the buyer backs out of the deal for any other reason, the seller keeps the hard money deposit.

The last thing a seller wants is to put the property under contract and have the buyer back out at the last minute because they couldn't raise enough capital. That puts them in a terrible position because they might have missed a better opportunity. Even if the next buyer is willing to renew their offer, they have to start the whole due diligence process over, and the closing will be delayed.

An aggressive offer with hard money on day 1 creates leverage in 2 ways: first, it shows the seller that you have full confidence in your ability to raise capital. Second, it reduces their risk in going to contract with you, because they will be compensated if you can't execute. I recently negotiated a sale with a buyer who offered $2 million in hard money for the initial EMD, and $3 million after due diligence. That's

$5 million in earnest money and the deal wasn't even that large, only $75 million in total. These buyers were offering 6% earnest money, and that was their offer *in the initial round*. We weren't even at the best and final stage yet. Nobody does that.

Normally, you try to keep your initial offer on the low side because the highest bidder sets the standard, and everyone else has to come up to meet them. Once you know roughly what the high bid may be, you can offer just a bit more to beat them out. These buyers were incredibly aggressive, and I knew they were absolutely set on buying that property. They won the deal.

Once you determine the best terms you could offer, you'll create a new LOI and email it to the broker. The best and final round will typically have 10 groups bidding. Sellers always say there will be only 2 rounds. That's never what actually happens. Ten gets cut down to 2 or 3, and you get one more chance to win the deal.

Best and Final, Final

Regardless of the seller's stated plan, you should always expect that there will be 3 rounds of bidding (I've occasionally seen it go to 4). They want to pump you for as much money as they can, and a bidding war is the best way to do that. The "best and final" isn't *quite* final, so you have a "best and final, final" round, too.

At this stage, you'll fill out a questionnaire to show your qualifications. The questions will include information about your operating group, like how many deals you've closed and how many properties you have in your portfolio. It will also include questions about your business plan, like how much you are underwriting for debt or taxes, and how you are structuring your deal for cash and IRR. They'll ask for references. The questionnaire is typically about 5 pages and very detailed.

After you submit your questionnaire, you'll have a buyer interview call with the seller and the broker. They'll ask about your group, your sources of equity, and follow-up questions about your answers on the form. They might ask you to explain your underwriting assumptions or how your research led you to make certain projections about the rents you can achieve. Basically, they want to make sure you know what you're talking about and you aren't missing anything important that could cause you to back out in the middle of the deal. They want to know you can execute.

This hurdle can be very, very hard for new operators to overcome because they don't have any track record to point to. A key principal or guarantor can be a valuable resource at this point. They should be on the call with you, because you won't just be drawing on their financial stability, but on their experience and knowledge. They can talk about the many deals they've been involved with and lend you their credibility.

After the interview, they'll ask you for another offer. At this point, you'll give the absolute best you can offer and still achieve your business plan. Then it's just a matter of whom the broker wants to work with and whom the seller wants to sell to.

If the seller finds your offer the most compelling, they will award you the deal and create a contract, the **purchase and sale agreement (PSA)**, that reflects the terms you specified. You'll wire the initial EMD into the escrow account the same day you execute the PSA.

Congratulations! You have the deal under contract.

You're Under Contract—Now What?

Once the deal is under contract, you're on the clock. You have a fixed deadline (usually 60 days) to get all the different pieces moving. If you haven't done so already, you need to engage with your real estate attorney, your securities attorney, your bank, your investors, your insurance company, and your lender. You need to create your SPE that will hold the property. You need to open a bank account for that SPE and fund it. You'll need to arrange insurance on the property and secure your loan. Most importantly, you need to introduce the deal to your investors and get their funds committed to the project. Let's look at each piece in order.

Your Single-Purpose Entity

In Chapter 1, you learned that the property you're acquiring will be owned by a business entity whose sole purpose is to hold and operate that multifamily community. Any lender for a multifamily deal will require that the property be held by a new, fresh entity with no pre-existing liabilities. Your first order of business once the property is under contract will be to work with your legal team to create that SPE. The paperwork for entity creation can usually be done within a few days, if not the same day. As long as you have a pre-existing relationship with a transactional real estate attorney, then you can get all those tasks done fairly quickly.

You'll need the incorporation documents as well as the tax ID (the EIN). Then you can set up a bank account. We have a relationship with a bank that handles our transactions, so we can easily mail the documents to our banker and they'll handle everything for us. I recommend that you look for a bank that can work with you on an ongoing basis because it makes everything easier.

Once the bank account is open, the investors can wire in their funds and you can make your earnest money deposit, pay application fees and third-party inspections, and pay the buyer at closing.

The Offering Memorandum

At the same time, you need to start preparing your investors. Remember the Project Funding Timeline I showed you in Chapter 4? You want to begin the process of securing capital as soon as possible by sending an email to your network of potential investors announcing the deal. This email will contain your offering memorandum.

The investor offering memorandum is extremely important. It's your opportunity to pitch your investors on your business plan for the property. You'll show them how you're going to take it from its current state and make money for them. You'll show the type of renovations and capital improvements you plan to make, how they will allow you to raise the rents, and ultimately how you will raise the NOI and the value of the property. Above all, make sure you clearly communicate the approximate date of closing as well as the funding deadline, which should be 3–4 weeks before the closing date.

Now is also the time to begin working with your securities attorney to prepare the PPM (private placement memorandum) for your investors, which they will receive after they express interest in the deal. You'll also move forward with your webinar, track your soft reserves, and follow up on all the other investor communications we covered in Chapter 4.

Insurance

Your next step will be to get quotes for insurance on the property. The lender will require that the property be insured, so your best guidance on how much and what types of insurance you need will be those lender requirements. Often your insurance broker will already be familiar with the various lenders' standard requirements. Once you get the quote or an insurance term sheet, you can send those to your lender for approval before you bind the policy. The insurance policy won't get bound before closing day (since you don't own the property until then). The day of closing will be the start date for the policy itself.

Debt

If you've done your underwriting properly, you'll already have multiple debt quotes for the deal so you can compare current interest rates, amortization, LTV or loan-to-cost requirements, and other terms. That gives you several options to weigh, and by the time you're under contract, you should be able to choose which debt option is best for you.

You can begin moving forward with application fees and third-party inspections to secure the loan, and the lender can move forward with their process as well. Once you engage with the lender, they will arrange a survey of the property, pull a title report to verify that the title is correct and unencumbered, and perform environmental inspections. Lenders usually take 30 days to approve a loan.

Securing Equity

After you send out your offering email, you should expect to get soft reserve commitments coming in from your investors—hopefully, you'll be getting some every single day. As the investors make those preliminary commitments, they'll get access to the PPM paperwork with full details on the deal, as discussed in Chapter 4.

Besides basic information about the deal, the PPM will include a number of forms and agreements for the investors to sign. They will need to verify that they are accredited or sophisticated investors. They'll need to read and sign the Subscription Agreement, their agreement to purchase shares in the SPE. The package also includes the Operating Agreement for the property. By buying shares in the SPE, the investors become members of the company. The Operating Agreement details the members' and the manager's rights and obligations, as well as the overall governance of the company.

Finally, the PPM contains instructions to set up direct deposit for their monthly cash distributions and wiring instructions to make their investment. Once they review those documents, they can immediately begin signing off on them and wiring funds into the SPE's account.

Due Diligence

During the first 30 days of the closing period, you will conduct due diligence on the property. Due diligence is your opportunity to verify that everything the seller has presented about the property is accurate, and there are no hidden issues or curveballs that could throw off your underwriting calculations or make the deal into a losing proposition. The first element of your due diligence is walking the units on the property. You (or in our case, our asset manager) will schedule time with the property management company to walk through every single unit in the community. You'll have a checklist for each unit, and you need to make sure that everything on that list is actually present in the unit as described. You'll look at the condition of the carpet and flooring, the countertops, cabinets and appliances in the kitchen, the bathrooms, walls, and ceiling. You're verifying that there was no gross misrepresentation of the physical condition of the property.

The next major element of due diligence is the lease audit. You will match the rent roll that shows how many units are occupied and what rent they are bringing in, against actual signed leases. You'll verify any concessions on rent or extra charges for amenities. Most of the time, the lease audit matches up very well. One discrepancy we see fairly often is when a resident has pets but isn't paying pet rent. Sometimes it's hard to determine that a resident has a pet if they are deliberately hiding it from the management. So that's when the unit walk and the lease audit can highlight discrepancies that you can correct and bring the property's income back up where it should be.

You want to get your due diligence done as quickly and thoroughly as possible, because if you put up soft money in the first EMD, it will go hard 30y days after signing the contract. The second EMD payment is due at the same time. If there's anything wrong, you want to know before you put any more money into the deal.

You can find a sample Investor Offering Memorandum, Private Placement Memorandum, investor emails, and checklists for your unit walks and lease audit in the Apartment Syndication Toolkit. Download it at PassiveInvesting.com/Toolkit.

A Team Effort

As you can see, there are a lot of moving parts during this closing period, and they all need to be happening at the same time. Your deadlines are tight. Sixty days is about 8 and a half weeks—and you want to have all your investor funds in place 3 to 4 weeks before closing. If you compressed your due diligence period to negotiate a fast closing, you have even less time than that.

Remember, as soon as you're under contract for one deal, you need to be finding the next one. As soon as your investors are committed, you need to be finding new investors. All the while you're hustling to complete a closing on time, you also need to have the bandwidth to keep feeding your pipeline of investors on one side, and your pipeline of deals on the other. Once you complete your first deal and start looking for the next one, you will have another full-time job keeping your hands full, too: managing your assets and operating your business.

It's hard. Trying to do it all on your own? Even harder. Theoretically you could find and close a deal on your own, but nobody can be in 2 places at once. You just won't be able to grow a sustainable, rewarding business as quickly as you could if you partner with someone else.

I always advise new operators to build a strong team so you can have each other's backs. You need at least 2 partners if you're going to do everything right. Three partners is even better because you can really separate duties and work together to get your deals across the finish line.

Look for partners with complementary skill sets. Our natural human tendency is to make friends and choose partners who are very similar to us. Personally, I am really interested in the investor relations side of things. I enjoy it. If I went out and chose partners who are all focused on investor relations, who would do the underwriting? Who would do the acquisitions and property improvement? People who don't like it as much—and that's not a recipe for success. And when it came to investor relations, you'd have 2 or 3 different people, each trying to do the same job in their own way. They'd butt heads. The partnership won't last.

I used to host a podcast called *Tough Decisions for Entrepreneurs.* The number one issue I saw, the toughest decision most entrepreneurs had to make, was when a partnership was failing and they had to figure out how to split up. When partners have complementary skill sets, the group has a much better chance at success than when everyone likes to do the same thing.

At the end of the day, this business is a lot more fun with a partner you can talk to and know that they're on your side. I talk to Danny so many times a day, I'm annoying. The great thing about our team is that we know how to do each others' jobs, so we can step in and help out if we need to. But on a regular basis, we have a very clear delineation of responsibilities, and we get to spend most of our time doing the things that interest us most. And if there's a big chunk of responsibilities that nobody loves to do, or nobody has time to do, you can hire that out.

This Deal and the Next

Remember the story about our very first acquisition? There's a sequel.

About a year after we closed that deal, I met with another private equity group out of Charlotte. They drove down here to Columbia, and over lunch one of the partners mentioned that property in Greenville by name. He said, "That was you, right?"

I said it was, and he went on, "I really hate you. You guys got that deal for $8.9 million. We were $20,000 less than you."

When he said that, I got chills running through my body. If we hadn't listened to our mentor and had tried to cut our offer price, I know we would have reduced it by more than $20,000. There was someone else right on our heels who would have been happy to take that deal, and we would have lost out. So if you distill everything we're teaching you about becoming an operator into a single principle, it's the same thing our mentor said: think long-term.

Finding, bidding, and closing deals takes an enormous amount of focus and preparation. Conducting successful negotiations requires you to understand all your options and how they'll affect your bottom line, so you can make clear decisions and respond quickly. It can be nerve-racking and sometimes very emotional. But through it all, you have to stay mindful that winning this bid isn't the goal—achieving your business plan is the goal, and that dictates what you can offer. On top of that, this deal isn't the only deal. You must conduct your business today in such a way that you can continue being successful—even more successful—tomorrow.

With that in mind, let's imagine your celebration when you close your first deal. And then, just like in real life, it's time to turn the page and begin the work of operating your multifamily asset as a profitable business venture.

Part 3

Operating the Business

As in Part 2, this section will be most relevant for you if you're an aspiring operator, intending to take an active role in owning and managing multifamily properties. If you're a passive investor, you might be interested in the discussion of tax strategy in Chapter 11. Otherwise, the nitty gritty decisions that an operator makes in order to reposition a property within the market or manage incremental income and expenses aren't really relevant to you—you just want to see the results, right?

For you passive investors, it's crucial to vet and analyze the operator you choose to invest with. That's what we'll cover in Part 4, so passive investors can skip ahead to learn everything you really need to know.

In this section, you'll learn:

- Chapter 9: Managing Your Physical Asset
    - How to add value to your property with strategic capital expenditures and upgrades
    - How to increase revenue through rent and monetized amenities
    - How to manage your major expenses

- Why experienced property management is crucial to success
- Requirements for effective property management
- The roles and responsibilities of your property management team
- The relationship between asset management and property management

- Chapter 10: Managing Your Financial Asset
  - How to oversee your property manager to ensure the asset's performance
  - Strategies to assist your property manager with marketing to residents
  - How to determine the right time to hold, refinance, or sell your asset

- Chapter 11: Tax Strategies as an Operator
  - Strategies for planning your acquisitions, capital expenditures, and sale of assets
  - How to use depreciation to maximize your revenue
  - How like-kind exchanges can help you manage your taxes
  - How to make the most of multifamily investing in your personal estate plan as an operator

Chapter 9

Managing Your Physical Asset

Brandon Abbott and Danny Randazzo

Closing on a new property is cause for celebration. There's always so much to do in the run-up to closing day that having everything finalized almost feels like a letdown. But you can't afford to rest on your laurels. Now that you own the property, it's time to make it profitable. You'll achieve that in 2 ways: the strategic choices you make with your capital expenditures and property upgrades will increase the value of your asset over time. Managing the property well on a day-to-day basis maintains your net income at the correct levels to deliver regular monthly returns to your investors and achieve your target price when it's time to sell.

In this chapter, Brandon will discuss property improvements that will have a long-term payoff by raising the property's value. Then Danny will show you how to effectively manage the property's operations so that they generate ample, consistent cash flow for your investors.

Adding Value to Your Property

Back in Chapter 2, Danny mentioned that one of the most powerful aspects of apartment syndication as an investment tool is forced appreciation. An operator has the opportunity to increase the value of their investment by the choices they make to improve and manage the physical property. We never buy a property and just hope that it will be more popular in 5 years' time and the value will go up all by itself. We take action to increase the value directly.

In Chapter 2, you learned the relationship between NOI (net operating income) and property value. The value of a multifamily property is somewhat influenced by comparable properties in the area, but ultimately the property's value is determined by the net income it generates. The higher your NOI, the more valuable your asset will be. That's why properties that could be performing better with the right upgrades and management are referred to as "value-add." There's room to make changes and add value in several ways.

Your goal in managing your physical asset is to increase its NOI. There are 2 avenues to improve NOI: increasing top-line income, and decreasing or optimizing operational expenses. When you're looking at revenue and expenses, the amounts we're dealing with sound small compared to the dollar amounts we're dealing with in acquisition. But you have to remember, these are recurring charges, scaled across many units or all the units in your property. A $5 per month fee, or $100 wasted at turnover gets multiplied by every unit in your community. When you're looking at 150 or 300 units over a holding period of 5 to 7 years, it all adds up quickly. So let's start with strategies to generate top-line income.

Increase Your Income

The most obvious way to increase revenue from your property is to raise the rent. Our product is housing—that's what we sell. The residents are our customers. If we can charge more, then we will have more money coming in.

Whether or not we can charge more without losing customers is a function of supply and demand. We have to make sure that our product is worth more to our customers. Otherwise, they'll go elsewhere and settle for a cheaper product. We justify a price increase by delivering a higher-quality product and a better customer experience.

Another way for a business (any business) to increase revenue is to add upsells and cross-sells to their product line. In our industry, that takes the form of add-on services and amenities. Let's look at different options to increase the value you deliver to your residents and opportunities to create revenue.

INTERIOR UPGRADES

When you buy a car, you could get a Ford Mustang V6 base model with no options, or you could get the Cobra package. You'll pay more for the upgrade because it has the features you want. In the same way, we look at our local market to see what type of interior features and experience our competition offers in order to plan attractive renovations that will fetch a higher rent.

We can judge which details are worth investing in based on the rents our competitors charge. Market rent is very important, but you have to pay attention to the finishes the competition uses, or you're missing a key piece of the puzzle. If similar properties are getting $1,000 a month for a one bedroom with granite countertops, luxury vinyl plank floors, stainless-steel appliances, and brushed-nickel fixtures, then you can't expect the same rent if your units have laminate counters, wall-to-wall carpet, basic white appliances, and dated brass fixtures. Customers will choose the more up-to-date, luxurious property in order to get more for their money. What do your competitors have that you don't have? That's where you'll find your best upgrades.

DEFERRED MAINTENANCE

If the previous owner of the property deferred maintenance and the condition is starting to go downhill, you have a great opportunity to reposition the property. Broken railings, rotting fascia boards, damaged gates, cracked parking lots, or peeling paint show that the property is neglected. Residents and potential renters will feel that the place is sketchy or possibly unsafe.

When you pressure wash the buildings, paint them, fix the gates and railings, and make everything nice and shiny, you're increasing the community's curb appeal. Repainting a dated color scheme to something more contemporary makes a difference, as does replacing signage that's dated or showing heavy wear. You might even upgrade vinyl siding to HardiePlank or stone veneer in order to make a big change in the buildings' appearance and desirability. Resurfacing and repainting the parking lot makes the place look really sharp. When you give people a good feeling about the space, they will value it more—that can increase your occupancy and allow you to raise rents.

Pay particular attention to the condition of the roof before you buy a property. Roofs are my personal specialty. I always inspect the roof for signs of wind or hail damage, and we make the seller file a claim on their insurance before they sell because it happened during their ownership. Then the insurance will pay for new roofs before we even take over the property, which could run to $300,000 or $400,000. It takes some work, and you might get a bit of a fight from the insurance company, but it allows you to instantly add value with no money out of pocket.

TECHNOLOGY

Smart home technologies are relatively new in the multifamily space, and they offer great opportunities for growth. Options like Google Home, Ring doorbells, or Nest cameras increase residents' feelings of security and convenience. In many large properties, the units may have direct access from the stairwell without a lobby or corridor to provide additional screening. Having a doorbell camera allows the residents to see who's at the door without walking downstairs. A smart thermostat can allow them to control the temperature from their phone to save on their energy bill. A smart door lock means they can lock the door remotely after their child leaves for school. These features are becoming very popular, and many residents are willing to pay a monthly fee to access them. If top-of-the-market rents are $1,000 a month, a $25 technology fee is very reasonable.

Internet access can be provided in a couple of different ways. One option is to make an agreement with the local provider (Comcast, Spectrum, or whoever it may be). We offer their service exclusively on the property in exchange for an upfront fee—$130 a month per unit is typical. Then the provider will also pay us a revenue share of the monthly fees from each resident, which is usually 10% to 20% of those monthly charges.

The other approach is to bring in our own internet service and become the provider ourselves. We pay to run the fiber-optic cables and sell the service directly to residents. By paying the upfront cost of installation, we get to keep 90% of the monthly fee from our residents instead of the 10% to 20% revenue share under the other model.

Right now, some of our properties use one model and some use the other. It largely depends on location and how difficult it is to bring in the infrastructure. More and more properties are moving toward the direct model as WiFi and streaming entertainment become more popular and cable TV and internet are less prevalent. If your demographic trends older or more blue-collar, they will be more likely to want cable TV. White-collar Millennials consider cable a waste of money as long as they can get fast streaming services for Hulu or Apple TV.

RECREATION

Whether your property would benefit from a lane pool, a volleyball court, fitness center, or dog park entirely depends on your local geography, your market demographic, and your typical resident profile.

Dog parks can be a great draw in certain markets. The park itself isn't really something you can monetize, but it can make the property more attractive to your target demographic. See how many pets are already on the property and consider where the property is located. In a more urban area, residents will probably appreciate a nice place to take their dogs. In a suburban location with plenty of open space around, installing a dedicated dog park might be a waste of money.

We've acquired a couple of properties that had a dated mix of recreation areas. In the 1990s, beach volleyball and jacuzzis were trendy, so we see a lot of communities with a sand volleyball court, a whirlpool, and a relatively small pool for the number of units. These days, nobody wants to get together with their neighbors in 100 degree heat and play volleyball in the sand, and communal jacuzzis are just gross. (Not to mention the shenanigans that go on in hot tubs—they can really become a problem).

Tennis courts are another ubiquitous '90s holdover. Here in the Southeast, unless you're in a town with a college whose main sport is tennis, those courts rarely get used because it's just too darn hot to be out there on the court in the middle of the day. Even in places where the sport is popular, there may be a big tennis club where people like to meet up. The college or club courts also tend to be better maintained than the smaller courts at an apartment complex. We want to cater to the majority of our residents. If 5% of the residents are tennis fanatics, that still leaves 95% who aren't using the outdoor space.

In our communities, we often turn those courts into "rooftop spaces" with turf grass, party lights, a fire pit, shaded seating, and some lawn games like cornhole boards. You might add a pavilion with a grill. Sometimes we'll also put a fenced playground near the pool and the rooftop space. This creates a very welcoming area for families to relax, swim, and watch the children play.

At first, we considered upgrading to a lane pool because there was a very nice fitness center, and it might be a good addition. After checking the resident demographic, we found there were a lot of retired people with pets. Instead of spending $150,000 on a lane pool that 25% of residents would use, we spent $30,000 to replace the volleyball court with a dog park that 80% of residents would use.

However, another property in Charlotte with a younger demographic was a bit smaller—a boutique deal with about 100 units—and had no pool. We added a lane pool because the residents would use it, and it really stood out from comparable communities.

For properties that abut a greenway with running or biking trails, it's common to find bike lockers or bike rentals. A secure storage area for residents' bikes is easy to set up, and for a minimal monthly charge (maybe $5 a month), you can bring in a little extra revenue. Residents or their guests might want to go biking even if they don't own a bicycle. Renting bikes for $25 a day or so allows them to take advantage of your prime location.

SHARED AMENITIES

There are a number of amenities you can add or upgrade in your property's common spaces that can increase your overall value. There are two strategies for planning these amenities. On one hand, you could offer them freely to residents as an all-inclusive experience. With this approach, you are positioning the property as a high-end, desirable place to live, and you'd raise the rent accordingly. On the other hand, you could use these amenities as a source of revenue by having residents pay per use. In this model, you would not raise rents quite as much, but having these options available can still make your property more attractive.

Car wash stations are a popular choice for multifamily properties. If you make the station completely free for residents, make sure your property manager is monitoring the water use. A leaking hose can put a big dent in your utility bill, while tightening up on waste in shared areas can be a great way to control expenses and add value in the long term. They can also be a useful source of revenue if you add a payment method on the vacuum or the water. Upgrading an older, free vacuum to a new one with an air compressor and a card payment system will cost you a little capital, but it can increase your NOI at the end of the day.

For properties with a lot of pet owners, a dog wash station can be just as popular. We take it a step further by adding a pet product vending machine. Nobody wants to bother carrying their dog shampoo up and downstairs if they can swipe their credit card and get a single-use packet for $2.00.

In the post-COVID world, more people than ever are working from home at least part of the time, so coworking spaces are becoming more and more popular. If the kids are home for the summer, or residents need to get out of the house to be able to focus, a quiet cubicle can be a great alternative. You can set up cubicles, hot desks, or a meeting room in the clubhouse and put a coffee machine nearby. Depending on the type of space and the expectations of your market, you might provide a simple workspace as a free amenity, but that's rapidly becoming obsolete. If you've invested in building out private spaces or meeting rooms, it's easy to set them up to have residents swipe a card and pay by the hour.

Concierge services can notably upgrade your residents' experience. A lot of delivery services won't take packages to the individual units. They can shave a few minutes off their route by dropping everything at the office. Unfortunately for the residents, that often means the office is closed by the time they get home, so they can't get their shipment until the next day. And when they do deliver to your doorstep, there's always the chance it might get stolen. Secure package rooms can solve both problems. The resident receives a door code when the package arrives, and they can access the locker 24/7 with the code. With a climate-controlled room and a refrigerator, perishable food or flower deliveries won't go to waste either. The convenience for residents is more than worth a small monthly fee.

Concierge dry cleaning can work in a similar way. The resident leaves their clothes in a locker, and swipes their card or logs into an app. The cleaner picks everything up and returns it back to the locker. The dry cleaners will offer you a revenue share for the exclusive license, so that creates another source of revenue.

For your laundry center, or any vending machines you might have on-site, make sure you have payment options that take cards and phone payments like Apple Pay. We have one property that used to have a standard soda machine and a digital payment machine. The digital machine would be empty halfway through the week because nobody carries cash with them anymore—especially not coins. As a matter of fact, the laundry center is a great place to put vending machines for detergent, dryer sheets, or even snacks.

Your overall strategy of whether to include or monetize amenities should be governed by the type of property you have, the demographic, and where your rents fall in the market range. Residents in a luxury property want a one-stop shop with everything included, and they're willing to pay more rent to get it. In a Class B property, or where your rent is already near the top of your market, it makes more sense to offer pay-on-demand options. Remember, you have to make a competitive offer and draw people in before you can wow them with an amazing site tour. If your rents are $100 more than your competitors, people shopping for an apartment will skip right over you, so you have to be careful with your positioning. Compare your property to your competitors—your residents will.

Reduce Your Expenses

All these avenues for increasing revenue from your property are only one factor in the NOI equation. Uncontrolled operating expenses can drain your revenue, so getting those expenses in line will maximize the benefit of the changes you're making to the property. Let's look at some common problem areas where you can make a big impact on your property's bottom line.

MARKETING

Marketing is a necessary expense because you have to attract residents before you can rent to them (and many of the improvements you're making to the property will be great marketing draws). However, ineffective or poorly directed marketing can be a huge waste of resources. First, take a look at how much the property managers are spending for marketing overall. Is it reasonable and proportional to the property's income? We use a rule of thumb that at our Class-A rental rates, marketing should cost about $200 per unit annually. Then look for ways to target the marketing more precisely as well as ways to make the marketing more effective at lower cost. Try different types of marketing, measure their success rates, and then use the strategy that works best for your market.

UTILITIES

Managing utility costs can greatly contribute to your cost-reduction strategy. You will most likely have one water meter for the whole property, rather than individual water meters to each unit. You can bill back the water usage at a flat rate according to the size of the unit. If you can find ways to reduce your overall water cost, you can keep the bill back at the same level and find some additional revenue, so there's a modest benefit there.

For example, smart home technology can include leak detection that ties into the management office. If there's a water leak, the water can be shut off automatically to avoid damage. That can save on your insurance bill as well as the water itself. If you audit each building's water use to see how the averages line up, you can detect and solve expensive problems. We had a property where a couple of constantly-running toilets were costing $3,000 a month. That was an easy fix that saved a lot of money. You can also cut back on regular usage by installing low-flow shower heads and toilets.

You can often earn credits from the power company or even from your lender by reducing energy usage across the property. For example, your exterior lights should be on a timer. Common areas like the laundry room or package room don't need to stay lit all the time, so motion-sensor lights can be a good option. You might convert all the light fixtures to LED instead of incandescent bulbs. Sometimes the power company will make those conversions for free, and you might save half a point on your loan's interest rate. Your residents will pay their individual electricity bills directly to the power company, so saving money makes them happy, too.

MAINTENANCE AND STAFFING

Whenever a resident moves out, you'll need to do turnover maintenance on the unit before the new resident moves in. Those recurring costs can build up over time. Some of your interior renovations and upgrades can also help you reduce turnover costs. For example, replacing carpet with LVP flooring eliminates the need to shampoo the carpets.

When we discussed acquisitions in Chapter 8, I recommended that you check into your staffing levels and the staff's effectiveness. Now that you own the property, you can implement your cost-saving strategies. If the previous management kept 3 full-time maintenance staff, you might be able to work equally effectively with 2 full-time people and 1 part-time groundskeeper. That could save you $30,000. If you own 2 properties close together with the same property manager, the management company could employ the same staff to cover both properties and split their salaries between the 2. Payroll expenses are a big chunk of your budget, and you want to make sure the work is done and the money spent as efficiently and effectively as possible.

The same holds true for your office administration, leasing agents, and other expenses of the property manager themselves. Every business has a budget—look for places you can trim without compromising on the services you deliver.

Boost Your Bottom Line

Adding value to your property is always a matter of raising your NOI. Through careful planning of your capital expenditures, you can upgrade the property's perceived value and your residents' quality of life. People are willing to pay more to live in a nicer community. They're also willing to shell out usage fees for convenient amenities. Give the people what they really want, and they'll happily pay more for it. Controlling your operating expenses leaves more of that revenue in play, so your NOI gets an even bigger boost. Together, these factors create long-term value for your investors.

Several of the strategies I mentioned will require you to work closely with your property manager since they will be handling all the day-to-day operations on-site. I'll hand it over to Danny to give you a broader and deeper look at how your property manager can help you deliver on your business plan.

Managing Your Property

Property management is an integral component to effectively managing assets and ensuring you meet the performance goals of your business model. Whoever you choose to oversee the property on a daily basis will interact with your residents and represent your interests. It's an extremely important role because the property manager not only ensures that the residents are well taken care of and that the physical asset stays in good shape, but they also have financial responsibilities. They must ensure that all income is collected and properly accounted for, expenses are paid, and the property performs as expected. As the operator, it's vital that you determine whether you should self-manage or work with a third-party management company to oversee the property.

DIY or Hire a Pro?

As a rule of thumb, I recommend that you work with a third-party company whose sole focus is property management. Because their business is 100% dedicated to a single specialty, they have the ability to stay up-to-date with ever-changing rules and regulations on the local, state, and federal levels that may apply to the residents, the staff, or the property itself. They will also stay apprised of new technology and trends in the industry. If you're interested in self-managing, you definitely need to have prior knowledge and experience managing residential property, keeping up with residents, and following landlord-tenant law.

There are well-established operating groups who establish a vertically-integrated property management division. I believe that new operators should focus entirely on mastering the syndication business and growing their staff for that business first. If you intend to acquire many different properties as an operator, trying to self-manage those properties will rob you of the time to seek new investment opportunities. Property management keeps the assets you already own performing, but it doesn't grow your business. For the operator, your business growth comes from growing your portfolio.

To underscore the point, let me show you a little bit of what it takes to manage a multifamily property well.

REQUIREMENTS OF GOOD MANAGEMENT

The ownership team's responsibility is to ensure the management team has the resources they need to effectively manage the property, and that they are using those resources to meet the goals outlined in your business plan. Those resources include professional management software, a marketing plan to attract new residents and lease units, and extensive knowledge of the local market to ensure you're charging competitive rents. Above all, you need great people on-site with smiling faces and friendly personalities to work with existing and prospective residents and make them feel at home.

You can choose from a plethora of property management software. If you work with an experienced third-party company, they will most likely have a system they prefer. Talk to them about why they selected the software they use. If you are self-managing, you should investigate which software will be most helpful and appropriate for your specific property and needs. Some of the most prevalent are Buildium, AppFolio, Yardi, and RealPage.

Dynamic rent pricing is a tool that can be implemented through your property management software. With dynamic pricing, the rental rates for an available unit change on a daily basis, similar to the way airline tickets or hotel room prices fluctuate daily. Dynamic pricing is a useful way to increase your NOI, and a qualified property manager will understand what it is and have experience using it.

As you implement your business plan, there is always a balance between raising rents and keeping existing residents. As with any business, getting new customers costs money, so the stability of your existing customer base has value. A good management company will have experience balancing occupancy rates versus the average rental rate at the property. Those specific metrics are both important to your total revenue.

ROLES AND RESPONSIBILITIES

For properties of 100 units or more, the property manager will typically employ on-site staff that includes the site manager, a leasing agent or consultant, a maintenance supervisor, and a full-time maintenance associate. For smaller properties of less than 100 units, you may only have a full-time manager on-site, or no full-time staff at all. For these smaller communities, the rental and management activities are handled in the back office and maintenance is done by subcontractors.

- The **on-site property manager** oversees the rest of the on-site team and acts as a liaison to the back office and the ownership team.

- **Leasing agents** or **leasing consultants** show units, take applications, and work with prospective residents. They report to the property manager.

- The **maintenance supervisor** reports to the property manager and is responsible for triaging and completing maintenance requests, as well as unit turnovers and routine upkeep of the property. Depending on the age of the property and the volume of repair requests, you may be able to use on-call maintenance and may not need a full-time maintenance supervisor.

- The **maintenance associate** reports to the maintenance supervisor and works to complete requests and routine upkeep as directed.

As you go up into 200 or 300 unit properties, you may need additional leasing agents and maintenance associates to keep up with the volume of work. As Brandon mentioned in the section on adding value, you should closely review how many staff you really need and which individuals are performing their roles effectively. You may find opportunities to trim or replace staff and improve your results.

Resident feedback is one of the best ways to gauge how the on-site staff and current management team are doing. I recommend that you check out reviews of the property on Google and at Apartments.com. It's always a good idea to interview the current staff to see whether you want to keep them on.

When you buy an underperforming asset, it can be advantageous to bring in a new on-site team instead of relying on the existing staff. Sometimes the low performance is due to the staff themselves, and sometimes the existing staff may not be willing or able to keep up with your planned changes. In that case, you'll need to search for, interview, and hire new people to fill those roles.

All these decisions need to be made and implemented quickly because your residents' needs don't stop during your takeover period. The day-to-day operations of the property need to continue as smoothly as possible—and as the operator, you will also be working on every other aspect of your business that we're covering in this book, all at the same time.

As you can see, property management at multifamily scale is a full-time job on its own. If you want to grow your business as an active investor and have thousands of doors—or thousands of assets—under management, your best option is to work with skilled third-party property managers instead of trying to do everything yourself.

Managing the Manager

When you work with a third-party property management company, your job is to manage the manager. This oversight falls under the umbrella of asset management. A third-party manager will typically charge between 2.5% and 5% of monthly gross income for a larger property, over 100 units. For properties smaller than 100 units, you can expect fees anywhere from 5% to 15%.

Good asset management—meaning a good working relationship with your property manager—begins before you purchase the property. When we're acquiring a property, we work well in advance with our third-party management company to make sure they are comfortable with the business plan and prepared for the changes that will come into play when we take possession of the property. They know the property's layout and condition, and we work together to create a plan for takeover. We have an ongoing relationship with a property management company that we always use. As a new operator, I recommend that you interview the existing property manager with an eye to keeping them on. You should also interview a few others to ensure you find the best management for your asset.

As I discussed in Chapter 8, you should request a pro forma budget from the property manager when you're preparing an offer, compare that to your own projections, and have follow-up conversations with the property manager as you refine your business plan and create your takeover plan. You should have extensive talks with the property management about occupancy, rental rates, and the potential to push rents. If there are significant discrepancies between your plans and the property manager's pro forma and you can't resolve them, that's a bad sign that your business plan may not be achievable. Make sure you and the property manager have full confidence in your plan before you proceed.

As soon as we close on the property, we'll set up daily or weekly asset management calls to review any open questions between the ownership team and the property management team. Those calls continue until both teams feel the property is stabilized from the takeover. At that point, we can reduce the frequency of those calls from daily to weekly, or from weekly to biweekly, depending on your needs and management style.

If your management company constantly misses deadlines, such as regular performance reports, or is slow to respond to requests like daily traffic information on applicants, it's important that you raise those issues. You need to communicate openly and effectively. If clear, regular communication and the resources you provide don't help the management team meet expectations, then you have a duty to your investors to find a new team that can deliver on your business plan.

If you're thinking about replacing the existing management company, I recommend you interview 5 to 10 different companies to find the best choice for your property and your business philosophy. Always ask for references from other owners they work with, and check up on those references to verify the kind of job they're doing for other properties.

A thorough and diligent approach to asset management gives you insight into the property manager's working style and business philosophy so you can identify any misalignment. If your approaches are not aligned, the property manager—and therefore the asset itself—will not perform up to your expectations. It's your responsibility to make changes to ensure that alignment of interest is corrected. You need the ownership team and the property management team working in tandem to deliver the best possible returns for investors, while also ensuring residents are comfortable and well taken care of in their homes.

Physical Choices, Financial Impacts

Every decision you make about your physical asset—from your initial underwriting and CapEx planning, to choosing a property manager, to replacing light bulbs—has an impact on your business's bottom line. You also have important choices to make about your big-picture financial strategy. That includes the way you manage the SPE that holds the property, the choices you make in selling the asset, and tax strategies that can protect your profits for the future.

You'll learn to understand and navigate those decisions in the next chapter, Managing Your Financial Asset.

Chapter 10

Managing Your Financial Asset

Danny Randazzo

As we discussed in Chapter 1, your multifamily business consists of 2 types of assets: physical and financial. The physical apartment community has value, generates income, and needs to be actively managed in order to perform properly. So does your financial asset. Remember, you don't personally own the property. The SPE you created owns the property, and you and your passive investors are shareholders of the SPE. Therefore, managing the business of the SPE is a larger undertaking than simply managing the property itself.

Good management of your financial asset has 3 main elements: overseeing your property manager; planning and executing the sale of the asset at the right time for the right price; and creating a solid tax strategy to make the most of your returns. In this chapter, we'll look at best practices for overseeing the property team and choosing when to sell.

Asset Management

In my earlier discussion of property management, I encouraged you to work with a third-party manager so you could focus on your business at a higher level. I also demonstrated the importance of establishing a productive relationship with the property manager early in the underwriting process.

Once your deal is closed, you will depend on your property manager to help execute your business plan. You should keep in particularly close contact during the takeover period, and then continue with regular check-ins throughout your holding period. I recommend that you set up a system of monthly and weekly reporting so you can understand how well your business operations are tracking your business goals.

Managing by the Numbers

Once a month, the property's financial reports are due. These include the current rent roll and the T-12 financial statement, so you can see how much total income was generated by the property and the expenses that are being paid. These reports tell you where your NOI is standing for the month, so you can distribute your monthly cash flow payments to your investors. The investors will also receive a copy of both reports, so they know exactly how their investment is performing. You can learn more about the rent roll and T-12 in the section on underwriting in Chapter 6.

Once a week—for us, it's always the first thing Monday morning—you should receive your property manager's **KPI (key performance indicator)** report. This report, which encompasses your most important statistics for the previous week, will set the tone for your week—hopefully, a great week.

The KPI report is generated by the on-site property manager and reviewed by the regional property manager before it gets submitted to us. For our business, the key indicators include:

- Weekly occupancy statistics

- Occupancy trends for 30, 60, and 90 days

- Total units preleased

- Garage, carport, or storage unit occupancy

- Total average income per occupied unit

- Average occupied rental rate

- Previous months' total delinquency percentage of collections

- Delinquency for the current month

- Current collection percentages for the month

- Summary information on any eviction proceedings or tenants with payment plans

- If there are any special exceptions to eviction proceedings, like the CDC's COVID-19-related eviction moratorium, the report would include any pending evictions governed by that rule

- Any pending rental assistance programs

- Marketing statistics, including the number of tours in the past week

- Number of new leases signed

- Number of declined applications

- Net leases gained over the last week

- Any resident appreciation events completed last month or planned for this month

- If you are in the process of renovating units, the number of renovated units ready to lease, renovated units to date, and any renovations still in progress

- Breakdown of vacant apartments, such as model units for showings, units vacant and not ready to rent, units rent-ready but still vacant, and units leased but not yet ready for move-in

- Open maintenance tickets, whether there are any work orders open longer than 48 hours, and the reason why

The final section of the KPI report shows the occupancy and traffic statistics of the surrounding comparable properties. This gives a snapshot of the overall performance of your submarket for comparison.

You'll find a sample KPI report in our Apartment Syndication Toolkit at PassiveInvesting.com/Toolkit.

Most of the KPI data can be auto-generated by any good property management software, but we require property managers to make some manual entries as well so that the report has full context. We don't just want naked data, we want to have insight into what's going on at the property and within the submarket. The data along with human interaction gives us a better look at what's occurred in the past week and allows us to make more accurate projections about trends over the months ahead.

Asset Manager Calls

As I mentioned in Chapter 9, regular calls with your property manager are essential to keep the property's performance on track. During the takeover and stabilization period, you'll be talking to your property management team on a daily or weekly basis.

We like to schedule weekly calls on Monday afternoon or Tuesday morning. That gives us the time to digest those KPI reports and have a meaningful conversation with the property manager about their plans for the upcoming weeks, or to discuss any challenges or obstacles that they may be facing. Above all, you need to ensure that you and your property manager are on the same page and that the property is meeting (or is on schedule to meet) the goals of your business plan. Having a regular call time on the books helps make sure there are no delays in decision-making for the property.

Marketing Strategy

Your weekly and monthly reports, along with your regular check-in calls, set you up for success in overseeing and managing the manager at each of your properties. They allow you to identify any issues or challenges so you can work closely with the property management team and get the property back on track as soon as possible. Your performance and financial reports can help you flag problems, but to really understand them, you need to take a deep dive into the property operations.

One area that heavily relies on partnering with your property team is marketing. Marketing is the property manager's purview, and they should handle the logistics. As the operator, it's your responsibility to see that the marketing produces results. For example, if you set expectations with the investors that the property should be 95% occupied, but it is only at 70% occupancy, then you need to get more involved to ensure the marketing is done right. Your management company should be able to work from their local knowledge and experience. You simply check in from time to time to verify and manage performance and only step in if needed.

Your marketing efforts are both art and science. I mentioned back in Chapter 6 that underwriting requires you to think like a product designer to some degree. Marketing also requires a creative touch to understand your potential residents' needs, interests, and habits. You need to help them find you and then make your property appealing to them.

The most effective marketing channels will depend on your area and your target audience. For example, Apartments.com is a great method of marketing available units in properties that typically rent for more than $1,000 a month. Those will be located in urban or suburban areas, where potential residents are used to shopping, researching, and living their lives online.

In more rural areas with rents less than $1,000 a month, you'll probably need a more localized marketing method. That might be a local Facebook group, an ad on Craigslist, flyers posted in local businesses, or a physical "For Rent" sign out front. As an asset manager, you must understand the local options for reaching apartment hunters and match the right marketing opportunity to your asset. You and your property manager will work together to create and execute an effective marketing plan.

The science of marketing is in making sure you're advertising the right rents for your submarket and to your target residents. You need to thoroughly understand rental rates and rent comps. You might have the nicest units in the whole area, but if you charge too high of a premium, you'll never rent that unit.

Online rent comps are a great piece of technology that can help you calibrate your expectations and set the right price. You can find comparable listings on Apartments.com, or directly on your competitors' websites, to find information on pricing and availability. A good property management software can give you insight into the trends of your asset and the local market so you can price your units appropriately. When you're starting out as an asset manager, you can rely on an experienced property manager to help you understand which surrounding communities are truly comparable to yours in terms of age, size, amenities, and the quality of the units. You need to work with your property manager and make sure you aren't selling yourself short or demanding the impossible.

From closing day on your acquisition of the property, to closing day on your disposition of the property, your job as the operator is to oversee the asset's performance and ensure success for your investors. If you do your job well, you and your investors will enjoy regular returns of cash flow, as well as a healthy profit when it's time to sell.

Selling Your Asset

After you successfully acquire your property at the right price for your business plan and execute that plan over your holding period with diligent asset management, the goal is to find yourself with a stabilized asset that has strong occupancy, solid cash flow, and a strong NOI that has elevated the property's value. At that point, you have 3 options: hold the property, refinance it, or sell.

The decision to sell should not be taken lightly. You need to run the numbers and evaluate your net return to investors based on the estimated sale price. The net return will include your loan payoffs and closing costs, as well as any sort of lender exit fee you may have to pay, and the expense of winding down the SPE. The sale price must be high enough to ensure a net return that meets or exceeds the expectations you set for your investors in your offering documents, as well as the projected returns you need to receive as the operator and general partner. Let's walk through the different factors you should take into consideration when deciding what to do with your property.

Hold On

Once your asset is stabilized and providing cash flow, you are in an advantageous position. Your business plan is not complete until you sell the asset and realize the profits for your investors, but as long as the asset is performing, you aren't forced to sell.

Throughout your holding period, you should constantly evaluate sales and comps in your market, as well as BOV on your own property. I recommend you request BOVs on a quarterly basis, so you can track the value of your asset and the current cap rates of other properties in your submarket. For the broker, these opinions are a way of keeping their business relationship with you fresh and top of mind, so they'll provide these BOVs to you at no charge.

If the submarket is trading conservatively or isn't aggressive enough when you are ready to sell, you can always hold on to it a little longer and continue to generate cash returns for your investors. That's why it's important to build flexibility into your offering documents for investors. You don't want to be locked into selling the property at a specific time, because economic forces in your submarket and the prevailing interest rates are such important factors in timing your sale. If the market is currently down, it will most likely recover within 12 to 24 months. Built-in flexibility allows you to wait out that market cycle.

One of the factors to consider when timing a sale is the way your lender structures their exit fee. Some lenders charge a flat percentage fee if you pay your loan off before the expiration period in your loan agreement. Flat fees are typically between one-half and 1% of the loan amount. Alternatively, some lenders charge an exit fee based on yield maintenance. That means that if the interest rate on your loan is higher than the current market interest rate, you would owe the lender the difference. For example, if your interest rate on the loan is 5%, and the current market rate has gone down to 3%, you would owe the lender 2% of the loan balance for the remainder of the term. That could be a 6 or 7 figure penalty, which will certainly put a dent in your profits from a sale. You must understand and take into account all the terms of your loan when you make a decision about selling the property.

Your long-term strategy as a syndicator also informs your timing for a sale. You want to free up your investor's money (and your own) when there is a new and even better opportunity available for them. Your investors don't want their money sitting idle—that's why they chose to invest with you in the first place. If you don't have another deal in the works, you may want to hold that asset a bit longer.

Refinance

An alternative to a sale that can also generate returns for your investors would be to refinance the property instead of selling it outright. If the property value and NOI have gone up, you would be able to get cash back from this capital event and return equity to your investors while continuing to hold the property.

As Dan mentioned in Chapter 7, our group won't underwrite deals that rely on refinancing to make the business plan work. That's a risky proposition, and we take a much more conservative approach to underwriting. Interest rates are unpredictable, so if we can't make the numbers work now, we don't want to gamble that the Federal Reserve *might* swoop in and make the interest rates work in 3 to 5 years.

However, if you underwrite conservatively and interest rates go down anyway, that can create a good opportunity. For certain properties and in certain economic climates, refinancing can be the best of both worlds. You want to evaluate the potential returns in each scenario to find the best choice at the time for your investors.

The Right Time to Sell

At some point during your holding period, you may be presented with a BOV that is equal to (or higher than) the projections in your original business model. This is your exit opportunity. Unlike the single-family housing market, there's no seasonal effect on timing your asset sale. You should sell your asset when you can get the best possible purchase price. If you've achieved your business model and you can achieve the returns set out in your business plan, then you're in a good position to sell.

The flexibility you build into your offering that allows you to hold the property longer than you expected can also allow you to sell early—as long as you can achieve your goal for returns. That opens up the possibility of moving your investors into a new opportunity that could be more advantageous for them and for you. There will always be market forces that you can't control, so trying to find the perfect moment to sell can be hard. Timing market cycles isn't the most important factor in choosing when to sell. You should sell when your goals for investor returns are met—ideally, when they're exceeded.

You can find more resources to help you understand when to refinance or sell, including video tutorials, in our Apartment Syndication Toolkit at PassiveInvesting.com/Toolkit.

Active Investing for Healthy Assets

Managing the financial side of your multifamily asset is an integral part of running an apartment syndication business that involves both day-to-day oversight and long-range planning. Overseeing operations, deciding when to sell, and making tax-savvy decisions can make or break the deal's profitability. Your investors are the shareholders of that asset, so it's your duty to manage their money responsibly. What's in their best interest is also in your best interest, so doing a good job at asset management also creates lucrative opportunities for you.

Chapter 11

Tax Strategies as an Operator

Dan Handford

As the old saying goes, there are 2 sure things in life: death and taxes. But just like staying physically active can help you live a longer, healthier life, being proactive about your tax strategy can help you hang on to your money longer and give you a healthier portfolio.

There are a number of tax advantages unique to real estate investing that you should build into your plans as an active investor, and that your passive investors will benefit from as well. First, we'll discuss the much-debated topic of Opportunity Zones. Then we'll dig into the most significant concepts you need to understand: depreciation, cost segregation, the power of the 1031 Like-Kind Exchange, and your status as a real estate professional.

Opportunity Zones (OZ)

Opportunity zones are a frequently-discussed topic in commercial and multifamily real estate. I wanted to give you my views and our group's philosophy on the potential tax impacts of investing in an opportunity zone.

The main purpose of opportunity zones is to encourage investment in economically distressed areas. For real estate in designated areas that are under economic distress, an investor's gains receive special tax treatment: investors may defer taxes on income from that property for the first 10 years of ownership.

We don't invest in opportunity zones, and we don't recommend them for a variety of reasons. From our perspective as investors, this tax deferment just isn't a very good incentive.

First, the provision expires in 2026. There just isn't enough time at this point to take full advantage of it. Next, these zones are designated in areas where the housing stock is dilapidated and median income is low. On top of that, in order to qualify for the tax benefit, you must invest CapEx into renovating the property that's equal to the purchase price minus the land value. So if you bought a property for $9 million and the land value was $1 million, you would then have to spend another $8 million renovating it just to qualify. Finally, properties in distressed areas are harder to sell so there's less upside for your exit.

The numbers simply don't work for a multifamily business. When you compare the effective returns on an OZ property against the effective returns on a property in a high-growth, high-income area, the business models can't compare. The returns on the high-growth property are better, even with a somewhat higher tax burden.

Opportunity zones are great for groups who are motivated to help a particular community turn around. They were created in order to make those turnarounds easier, and in that respect, they work. Financially, there's little benefit for an outside investor who is just looking for the best possible deal. If you are serious about this investing strategy, make sure you do your due diligence and understand what you are getting into.

Depreciation and Cost Segregation

If you're interested in investing in real estate, you may have heard of cost segregation before, but many people don't really understand what it means. If you've never tried to invest in real estate to offset your taxable income, then you've probably never heard of it at all. Cost segregation refers to the IRS provision that allows you to accelerate depreciation on your assets.

Depreciation generally means a loss in the value of a commercial asset over time due to wear and tear, like the normal life span of factory equipment or a fleet of commercial vehicles. When it's applied to real estate, depreciation allows you to spread out the cost of purchasing, improving, and maintaining the asset over the span of your holding period. This creates a tax deduction which can be used over several years to offset your taxable income from a real estate investment.

For example, if your real estate investment is generating cash flow at $5,000 per year, that's taxable income. However, if your depreciation on the investment is $20,000 per year, then you've offset your whole cash flow to zero. You can defer the taxes on that income until you sell the asset (unless you perform a 1031 exchange discussed in more detail below).

Here's the great part about depreciation: if the amount of depreciation you can claim is greater than your income from the property, that deduction doesn't just disappear. As a passive investor, you can use it to offset any other passive income you may have. If you can't use it, you can defer it to another year, and it will just keep rolling over and building up until you can use that deduction. As an operator, there are even more interesting things you can do with depreciation, and we'll get into that later on in the chapter.

There are 3 types of depreciation: **straight-line depreciation, bonus depreciation, and accelerated depreciation**.

Straight-Line Depreciation

If you hold a residential real estate asset, your depreciation is spread over a 27 and a half year schedule. In a commercial asset, it's a 39 year schedule. Multifamily properties are classified as residential real estate, so the shorter schedule applies. Here's how it works.

If you buy a $10 million property, immediately you subtract the value of the land. Land doesn't depreciate—only structures do. So if the land is valued at $1 million, then you have a $9 million asset that you can depreciate over 27 and a half years. That comes out to $327,000 of depreciation a year. That's a really powerful tax deduction! But it gets better…keep reading.

Bonus Depreciation

The first bonus depreciation was enacted in response to the lagging economy shortly after the 9/11 attacks. It was designed to spark the economy with new investments. In 2017 the bonus depreciation was set to start phasing out. Then-President Trump extended and increased the bonus depreciation amounts, which are now set to phase out starting in 2023 through 2026.

Bonus depreciation is a temporary tax provision that allows you to take 100% of the depreciation in year 1 on any renovations or property improvements performed in the first 12 months of ownership. So instead of accelerated depreciation, this is instant depreciation on those renovations. This is a great benefit for investors, and it also encourages owners to get their renovations done quickly instead of pacing them out over time.

Bonus depreciation has been used as a temporary economic stimulus measure in various forms and with various percentages since 2002, and the provisions normally expire within a couple of years. When you're ready to plan your first (or your next) multifamily deal, ask your tax advisor about bonus depreciation to see whether you could take advantage of it, because it would impact your CapEx and underwriting decisions up front.

Accelerated Depreciation

Now, certain items or parts of the property will depreciate faster than the building as a whole—things like toilets, countertops, and appliances, or large capital expense items like the roof or the asphalt in the parking lot. In real life, these things will wear out and need to be replaced in less than 27 years, and the law reflects that reality. So you can front-load the depreciation on those items, and take a larger amount of depreciation in the first 5–15 years that you own the property.

In order to claim accelerated depreciation, you need to have a cost segregation study done by a third-party engineer firm. They will inspect the property piecemeal and record every individual item that could qualify for accelerated depreciation: the cabinets, the flooring, the appliances and fittings, right down to the sheetrock and nails in the wall. Each item has a classification for its depreciation schedule, so the inspector will tally up everything that can be depreciated over 5 years, and everything that can be depreciated over 15 years.

So in our example, instead of taking $327,000 per year at a steady rate, you could take depreciation for the first 5 years at $575,000 or $750,000, depending on the findings of the cost segregation study. This is particularly significant for a multifamily investor. Our normal holding periods are between 5 and 7 years, and one of the main reasons for that time horizon is that it allows us to maximize depreciation for our investors and for ourselves.

Even better, the depreciation schedule runs from the moment you buy a property, so every time you buy a new asset, your depreciation schedule resets to year 1. You take 5 years of accelerated depreciation on Property A, sell it, and then you get 5 new years of accelerated depreciation on Property B. You only need to have the cost segregation study done once when you acquire the property. The study will include the schedule of everything you can claim on a 5-year cycle and a 15-year cycle, and your tax professional can follow that schedule when they figure your taxes. Cost segregation allows us to claim depreciation that we would never be able to use otherwise, and it gives tremendous tax benefits.

There are many different groups that can provide a cost segregation analysis for your property. We use a national firm, Madison SPECS.

Since a lot of the units in a multifamily property have the same layout and interior finishes, the engineer will visit 1 unit of each floor plan and calculate the depreciation for it. Then they multiply that by the number of similar units. It's not a cheap endeavor. You can expect to pay $5,000 to $10,000, depending on the size of the property, but the benefits are worth far more than the cost.

As the operator, you will provide the investors with a schedule K-1 tax form each year, which shows their share of all income and losses from the property, including depreciation, so they can claim their portion of the depreciation on their own taxes.

Depreciation, Basis, and Capital Gains

The thing you must bear in mind about depreciation is that it doesn't eliminate your taxes, it simply defers them until you sell the property. The IRS will recapture the taxes on that money eventually. The way that works is that depreciation reduces your **basis** in the property over time. Your basis is the amount you paid for the asset, so let's say you bought a property for $1 million, and that's your basis. Then the value of the property goes up, and you sell it for $1.2 million. The difference between your basis and the sale price is your **capital gain**, and that's what you're taxed on. So in this scenario your taxable capital gain is $200,000.

Sale price – basis = capital gain.

Now let's say that you take depreciation on the property to offset your income. In the first year, your cash flow is $100,000 in income and you claim $100,000 in depreciation, so you don't pay any tax on that cash flow. Remember, the tax doesn't disappear—it's just deferred. The depreciation reduces your basis, so now your basis on the property is $900,000. The same thing happens in the second year. You take $100,000 in depreciation, and now your basis in the property is $800,000.

Purchase price – utilized depreciation = basis.

So when you sell the property for $1.2 million, and your basis is only $800,000, then your depreciation recapture is $200,000 and your capital gain is $400,000. That's where the IRS recaptures the deferred tax. Currently, the depreciation recapture tax rate is 25% and the long-term capital gains tax rate is 15–20%. Fortunately, there is also a great strategy for dealing with capital gains taxes on real estate: the 1031 exchange.

1031 Like-Kind Exchanges

A 1031 exchange is a powerful tax deferral strategy that dates back almost to the beginning of the US tax code. It's named for the section of the tax code that created it, and the original version of Section 1031 allowed investors or business owners to exchange all sorts of assets with each other without generating taxable gains. If you wanted to exchange a business for another business, or a piece of real estate for another piece, you could defer paying capital gains until you eventually sold the asset for cash.

The provisions have been modified over time, and the current Section 1031 allows only like-kind real estate to be exchanged this way. That means that, instead of paying capital gains tax when you sell a multifamily asset, you could do a like-kind exchange and invest in a new property. As a matter of fact, you could keep on doing like-kind exchanges one after the other in a chain, and no capital gains or depreciation recapture tax would be due until you break the chain. Tax rules and strategies are constantly evolving, and we recommend you consistently check in with a professional tax advisor to ensure you are maximizing your benefits while following the law.

Qualified Intermediaries

An important part of the modern Section 1031 is that the exchange doesn't have to be simultaneous. You can sell the first property and buy the second property 6 months later—as long as you don't take possession of the money in between.

The proceeds from the sale are held by a **qualified intermediary (QI)**, sometimes called an **accommodator**, until the purchase of the next property. The intermediary must be a third party unrelated to you, but there are no specific licensing or other requirements as long as they are fully independent. Typically, you would hire a professional QI to hold the money in escrow and complete the necessary paperwork. We usually use a division of the Madison companies, the same group we hire for our cost segregation studies. Their QI division is called Madison 1031. There's another called IPX 1031, and many others you could work with.

When you decide to execute a 1031 exchange, you should engage your intermediary as soon as you go under contract on selling the property and sign the PSA. To work with an intermediary, you'll sign several agreements including a Like-Kind Exchange Agreement, an Escrow Account Agreement, and other documents that allow the intermediary to assign or accept documents, or otherwise fulfill their role in completing the transaction. When you sell a property, the proceeds are wired into the intermediary's account, and when you purchase the new one, the intermediary wires the funds into the new asset.

1031 Timeline

The timeline for a 1031 exchange is very strict. Once you sell an asset, you have 45 days to identify the next asset you plan to acquire. You can identify more than 1 replacement property. There are 3 different ways to identify replacement assets: the Three-Property Rule, the 200% Fair Market Value Rule, and the 95% Exception Rule.

SALE OF ASSET
PassiveInvesting.com decides to sell an asset. All investors are notified via email that the asset is under contract to sell.

YOUR DECISION
All investors receive a questionnaire to elect to 1031 exchange or liquidate the investment. If you decide to 1031 exchange, no further action is needed. If you decide to liquidate, you'll provide how you would like to receive your proceeds from the sale.

ASSET IDENTIFIED
Once the asset being exchanged into has been identified, we will notify you via email. This email will include the offering summary for you to review.

INVESTOR
Your return of initial investment + your share of the proceeds will be your investment in the new asset. You'll begin to receive monthly distributions from the new asset after the first full month of ownership.

THREE-PROPERTY RULE

This is the most widely used method because it's the simplest. You just need to identify up to 3 properties that you might exchange the funds into. Theoretically, you could wind up using the sale proceeds to purchase any or all of those 3 properties. In reality, the money normally goes into 1 property and the other 2 are just selected as possible alternates. That way, if your first choice of deal doesn't work out, you have other options.

200% FAIR MARKET VALUE RULE

With this method, you can identify more than 3 properties as long as their combined value is no more than 200% of the fair market value of the property you sold. So if you sold a property for $1,000,000, then you could identify as many properties as you like up to a total fair market value of $2,000,000.

95% EXCEPTION RULE

Under this rule, you can identify an unlimited number of properties, as long as you actually acquire at least 95% of the total value within the required time frame. This method is the least used because it is so much more complicated to execute. Closing one 1031 deal within the 180-day limit is complex enough. There are some circumstances when this rule might be the best choice, but for most people it's just overkill.

After you identify your replacement asset (or assets), you have 180 days from the original sale to close on it. It's essential that you complete the transaction within that 180 day period, or your exchange will be disqualified and you will be forced to pay capital gains tax on the asset you sold.

Multifamily Investing through a 1031

As an active or passive investor, you can place funds from a 1031 exchange into a multifamily deal, you can roll your proceeds from exiting a multifamily deal out to a 1031 exchange for your next investment, or both. An operator has to do some extra paperwork in order to accept 1031 funds into a deal, so it's common for there to be a higher minimum investment in that case. When we accept 1031 funds from an investor, we require a $1,000,000 minimum investment. The ability to defer taxes can make your multifamily investment an even better vehicle for long-term growth of your portfolio.

The Legacy Play

One of the most exciting possibilities for 1031 exchanges is the way you can use them in planning your estate. Remember, when you roll the proceeds from selling one asset into purchasing another, you can defer paying taxes as long as you keep the chain of 1031 exchanges going.

The longer you hold an asset and take depreciation, the lower your basis goes and the higher your taxes would be when you sell. However—and this is the big twist—when you die and the property passes to your heirs, they don't inherit your depreciated basis. Their basis for the property resets to its current fair market value. Even if you had depreciated that property to a basis of zero, your heirs' basis would be its full value on the day they received it.

That means that if they sold it immediately, their capital gains would be zero. No capital gains means no capital gains tax. Now, hopefully they won't sell. We'd love to see them hold that asset and continue to receive cash flow for a long time—I'm sure you would, too. But regardless of their future decisions, your strategic use of the 1031 exchange structure can turbocharge the growth of your estate and help create a wonderful legacy for your family.

There are many more layers of complexity to 1031 exchanges, such as how to deal with debt, differences in value between the old and new properties, what makes a property "like-kind" or not, and so on. There are entire books devoted to the nuances of the 1031, and we have several articles about them in our Knowledge Base at PassiveInvesting.com. If you're contemplating using a 1031 for the first time, talk to your real estate attorney and tax advisor.

Real Estate Professional Status

I mentioned earlier that passive investors can use depreciation to offset their passive income, even the income they receive from other passive investments. Active investors can leverage depreciation for even greater benefits if they qualify for the real estate professional status. With that status, you can use depreciation to offset all your income from any income source. That means that if you claim enough depreciation on the properties you're operating, even if you have ordinary income from other work, you could wind up owing zero federal income tax because none of that income would be taxable.

Qualifying for real estate professional status doesn't require any kind of special degrees or licenses. You simply have to prove to the IRS that you are spending 51% or more of your working hours as an active real estate investor, and that you spend at least 750 hours a year working in that position. That's roughly 15 hours a week.

This is another reason we don't recommend trying to become a multifamily operator as a side hustle while you work a full-time job. Technically, you could work 40 hours a week at a nine-to-five job and still qualify, but you'd have to work 81 hours a week, all year long. Maybe you can pull that off, but honestly most people can't—and the IRS knows that. So if you have a full-time salary coming in as well as claiming real estate professional status, that's a big red flag for an audit. Nobody wants that.

Maybe you don't care. You're willing to grind, and you aren't afraid of an audit because you know you did the work. That's fine, as long as you have your documentation in order, because the IRS will check. Most CPAs recommend that you keep a time log of every amount of time you spend working on your real estate business, so if need be you can pull it out for the IRS auditor and prove it. In fact, most CPAs will recommend you keep that log even if your wage-earning job is only part-time, or if you run another business. If there's any possibility at all of the IRS questioning your status, you'd better document your time.

Holding real estate professional status is a great benefit, because it means you can offset pretty much 100 percent of your income with depreciation. This offset only applies to federal income tax. Most states don't follow these rules. Even so, generating all the cash flow you have from your multifamily properties, plus any other business or work you may have, and being able to keep it free of federal income tax? It's a powerful tax tool.

Setting the Bar

For those of you who are primarily interested in becoming operators, the first 3 sections of this book contain all the basic concepts you need to understand in order to get started. Of course, there is always more to learn, and a world of detail involved in actually getting a project off the ground. We encourage you to join us at the MFIN (Multifamily Investor Nation) so you can continue your advanced education in establishing and growing an apartment syndication business.

The next—and final—section of the book is focused on the needs of passive investors, particularly on how to vet and select the right operating group to work with. Aspiring operators may want to read on so you can understand what's expected of you! We hope to set a high standard, because our investors deserve the best.

Part 4

Passive Investing

For those of you who are interested in passive investing, this section is focused on helping you form a thoughtful and coherent strategy for your multifamily investments, choose the operators and deals that can deliver on your investment goals (and avoid the ones that can't), and take advantage of the incredible tax benefits the multifamily business has to offer.

In this section, you'll learn:

- Chapter 12: Passive Investing Strategy
  - How to make sure passive (rather than active) investing is right for you
  - How to define your investing goals
  - The right time to invest in apartment syndications

- Chapter 13: Sound Operators, Sound Deals
  - Choosing the right operator (and avoiding the wrong ones)
  - How to read your offering documents and key items to look for
  - The features that make or break a deal as a quality passive investment

- Chapter 14: Building Wealth with Multifamily Investing
  - Tax advantages of multifamily investments
  - How to offset taxable income and defer capital gains
  - How Real Estate Professional status can benefit passive investors

Chapter 12

Passive Investing Strategy

Dan Handford

Multifamily investing—particularly my role in investor relations—is all about making connections with people. I want to spend this last section of the book making a connection with you, so let me give you some insight into my own experience getting started in the multifamily business.

I began as a multifamily passive investor before I ever made a move toward becoming an operator. My wife and I own a group of nonsurgical orthopedic medical clinics in South Carolina. Our income from that business was great, especially since the clinics are 100% debt free. The cash flow coming off was nice but it caused us a tax problem: we were writing large 6-figure checks to the government not once a year, but quarterly. It was very frustrating to work so hard building the clinics to see a large chunk of our profits being sucked out by Uncle Sam. This is what sparked my desire to start investing in real estate. So I sought out a real estate investment that could help us with our tax burden. Multifamily investing was a great solution because we could invest in high-quality assets passively and use depreciation to reduce our taxable liability. If you skipped directly to this section, I highly recommend you go back and read about the tax advantages of multifamily investing in Chapter 2 and Chapter 10.

Over the years, my wife and I have invested in over 80 different limited partnerships as passive investors. We've worked with about 18 different operating groups. I'm drawing on that experience to give you my best advice for planning your own strategy as a passive investor. In this chapter, I'll walk you through defining your goals for your overall strategy and the criteria you use to choose particular deals, how to determine whether passive or active investing is right for you, the role of timing and economic cycles in planning your investments, and the importance of ongoing education for every investor.

Passive or Active

Many of our members in the MFIN find us because they're debating whether or not to become active investors. I expect you might be reading this book for the same reason. There are a number of factors to consider as you find the right path for yourself: your education about the business, the amount of time you're able (or willing) to devote to the business, and how much support you will need from a team.

I recommend that anyone interested in multifamily investing begin learning about the industry by investing passively with an experienced and successful operator. It's a complicated endeavor, and there's a lot to learn—after all, we wrote this whole book about it, and we're just scratching the surface of many of the topics. Our own investors come to us with all kinds of questions throughout the transaction, and educating them is a big part of our business.

As a passive investor, you have the luxury of time to see all the aspects of a deal get worked out, without the pressure of executing them yourself. You can get hands-on experience with everything from reading deal documents, to initiating large wire transfers, to regular communications. If you decide later on that you might want to participate actively, you'll have many good examples of what to do and how to do it (and perhaps a few examples of what you don't want to do).

Next, you should ask yourself how you want to spend your time. As we discussed back in Chapter 1, building a syndication business (and doing it well) is a full-time job. Are you at a place in your life where you're willing and able to take on a second career? I often use the example of a surgeon who is already devoting 80 hours a week to their profession—they couldn't effectively scale a syndication business without abandoning a lot of their duties as a doctor. There just aren't enough hours in a week.

Things could change in the future—I've seen some of our investors in their 30s or 40s retire from their nine-to-five jobs, or perhaps you might want to step back from your current work when the kids go off to college. If you decide later on to become an operator, you always have that option and you'll have more experience under your belt. For most of our investors, they just want to know their money is working and get a distribution deposited so they can focus on other things.

Being an active investor is active. There are a lot of moving pieces, and even though each piece is not very difficult on its own, the sheer complexity of them becomes overwhelming. We recently hired someone just to keep track of the timelines of all the different transactions we're working on. There are dispositions, acquisitions, property tours, asset management, communications, and so many other tasks. We have over 50 people on our team now in 2023 to maintain our growth and protect our investors' money.

That raises another question: do you want to manage people? As an operator, even for a small property, you will need property managers or other help. When you have a property management team, you have to manage the property manager. In other words, you have to manage the manager. A syndication business needs to be run like a business, and that means 40, 50, or 60 hour weeks. Sometimes more.

Ultimately, choosing whether to invest actively or passively means choosing the lifestyle you want to lead. I love building my passive income, but I love building businesses, too. It's fun for me. If spending the next several years starting a time-intensive business from scratch isn't your idea of a good time, then passive investing will give you the stability and returns you're looking for, without all the hassle.

Define Your Goals

Once you've made the decision to approach apartment syndication as a passive investor, you need to set some parameters to help you find the right operators and the right deals for you. The key decision you need to make as an investor is what you want to invest in.

Some people want to invest in Class A properties in primary markets. Some people want to invest in new development, others are looking for value-add projects. You need to understand your own risk tolerance, as well as the type of returns you're looking for. When you know your box, then you can choose operators who are presenting those opportunities.

The first step in defining your investing criteria is to understand your own risk profile. Every well-balanced investment portfolio will contain a mix of low, medium, and higher-risk assets, but the right mix for you is a personal decision based on your needs, your time horizon, and your risk tolerance.

Multifamily real estate offers all of these options. Class A assets have the lowest risk, Class B is middle-of-the road, and Class C and D have the highest risk. The returns, as always, match the risk level: Class C and D have the highest potential returns, Class B has moderate returns, and Class A has the lowest returns—but Class A also has the most consistent cash flow.

You can refer back to detailed descriptions of the real estate asset classes and submarkets in Chapter 5.

When choosing your asset classes, it's crucial to understand risk-adjusted returns and the level of cap rate change between the classes. At the time of this writing, cap rates for Class C and Class B assets are so close together that there's not much benefit to choosing Class C. On paper, you might make a slightly higher return on Class C, but after you adjust for the higher risk, Class B makes more sense 9 times out of 10. You can't just look at the IRRs and compare the returns directly. You need to do your homework and adjust for that increased risk.

Beyond risk and return, consider how well the operator's business model meets your needs. What is the projected holding period for the deal? Do you need cash flow to subsist on throughout the holding period? If so, you probably want to look for a higher asset class that is stabilized or nearly stabilized. Do you prefer a big pop in your returns at the end? You might look at new development or major value-add projects.

Operating groups generally stick to a specific asset class or a fairly narrow range of asset classes within defined submarkets. They should also have well-defined goals of their own. For example, we invest in Class A to B communities in low-cap rate primary markets in the Southeast. Our risk profile is low, with conservative underwriting and a focus on cash flow for our investors. Other operators might focus on new developments, or on turning around higher-risk properties, or exploring different geographical markets. By investing with multiple operators who have different goals, you can create your optimal mix of risk and returns.

Large multifamily funds will create a custom portfolio for a single investment. They might raise 50 to 100 million dollars and acquire a couple of hundred million dollars' worth of assets in one big pool. You can mimic a fund like that for yourself on a small scale by cherry-picking the classes, markets, and operators you invest in. That way you can normalize your overall risk and return profile.

Within a specific deal structure, many operators offer 2 or more share classes. That allows you to diversify your risk within the same investment. You might choose Class A shares with preferred equity, where you minimize your risk and get higher cash flow, while forgoing a potential upside when the asset is sold. Then, in order to participate in the growth of value, you could also invest in Class B shares that have lower cash flow but a bigger piece of the pie at disposition. We discussed capital stacks at length in Chapter 7, and in the next chapter we'll address how to read and analyze multifamily offering documents so you can choose the right position in the capital stack.

The Right Time to Invest

I get a lot of questions about timing the market and where we are in the economic cycle. People want to wait for a downturn so they can get a better deal, or they worry about a downturn making multifamily less profitable. My answer is always the same: the best time to invest in real estate is right now. That's true in every type of market cycle. As a matter of fact, yesterday was too late.

I don't have a crystal ball, and I can't tell you what's going to happen in 6 months or a year. In 2018 and 2019, I was marveling at how hot the market was and how cap rates were dropping so rapidly. In the beginning of 2020 we didn't know what was going to happen in 6 weeks, when COVID-19 went from distant news to lockdowns everywhere, seemingly overnight.

The beautiful thing about real estate is that time resolves a lot of problems. In 2021, we saw a hot market again. We had deals that we were planning to hold for 7 years, that we sold 1 or 2 years later after we purchased because properties we bought at $52 million were getting offers of $79 million, which is nuts.

A hot market often makes people concerned about inflation. In fact, wage inflation helps real estate quite a bit. When residents make more money, we can charge more rent. As rents go up, the NOI of the property goes up, and if cap rates stay the same, it increases the value of the asset. As a consumer, I don't want to see high inflation. But if it's going to happen, I want it to be after I buy more real estate.

If you skipped to this section or need a refresher, you can find an in-depth discussion of NOI and asset valuation in Chapter 5.

Timing the market is hard, so the best strategy is to mitigate your risk anytime you invest. Don't commit to multiple deals where you're

90% leveraged and just hope it all works out. You also need to make sure that when you compare deals, you're comparing risk-adjusted returns. Some deals look great on paper but carry very high risk. In the worst-case scenario, where some massive market boom or crash caused real estate valuations to plummet, you have to rely on the quality of your underwriting. If the deal was underwritten properly and the asset has ample operating reserves, then you can maintain the asset through any kind of downturn. In the last 100 years, no recession has lasted longer than 18 months. As long as you can leave your money in a stable asset, you can ride out that downturn and things will get better.

Beyond the issue of returns or value, you also need to look at the tax benefits of multifamily real estate. The tax code is very favorable to real estate investors right now, and that's one thing that can change significantly from one administration to another. A lot of politicians own real estate, so that might mitigate any sweeping changes, but the political climate is just as significant (if not more significant) than the economic climate. If you wait for the perfect time, and suddenly capital gains tax goes from 25% to 50%, or the 1031 exchange provision gets scrapped, then you might miss out on some of the major benefits of passive investing.

If we could fast forward to the year 2025 or 2026, most likely you'd be sitting there wishing you'd invested earlier. I know operators who didn't buy anything in the last 2 or 3 years because they thought everything was overpriced. They're calling me now saying, "If only I hadn't sat still so long!" Everything in life carries risk. The key is to choose smart risks.

Never Stop Learning

The most important thing you can do to accelerate your growth as an investor—and accelerate the growth of your portfolio—is to spend time getting educated about your options. In order to make smart strategic choices, you need to understand the industry as well as understanding how to optimize and protect your gains.

There is so much information available on the internet that people take it for granted. Ten years ago, you'd spend thousands of dollars for the knowledge and insight you can pick up these days for free on webinars and blog articles. Don't miss out, because these opportunities can make a huge difference in your success as an investor.

Get to know your operators. Get to know other investors. Work that network for referrals and recommendations to find the best resources and the best investment options. Knowledge and thoughtful choices will help mitigate your risks and maximize your returns.

Let's continue that education right now in Chapter 13: Sound Operators, Sound Deals.

Chapter 13

Sound Operators, Sound Deals

Dan Handford

You'll often see operators and passive investors referred to as general partners and limited partners, and I want to emphasize that it really is a partnership. Operators and investors need each other in order to make a deal come together, and each of those roles is very important. You must be able to rely on each other because you have a common goal.

I believe that educated investors make the best partners, and they're able to choose the best partners. That's why we're going to address the red flags that will guide you away from subpar operators or bad deals, and toward reliable general partners who put together strong investment opportunities. I want to give you confidence, clarity and comfort about how to review offering documents and make a decision on wiring money to an operator that you may not have had any face-to-face contact with.

In this chapter, we'll cover how to vet an operating group, how to efficiently review and analyze multifamily offering documents, and how to choose deals that fit your investing goals.

Choosing an Operator

In the last chapter, we discussed how to set your personal investing criteria, because that will narrow down the field of operators to help you find the right match. When an operator's goals and interests are aligned with your own, it sets the stage for a mutually beneficial relationship.

Let's take a look at the steps you'll need to take to properly vet a general partner and choose the right operating group to invest with. (And for you aspiring operators who may be following along, these are the criteria investors will use to vet you!)

The most important qualification to look for in an operator is experience. Multifamily is a very attractive business, and there's a constant influx of new operators who are eager to participate. However, it's also a very complex business—so complex that we release a new educational video every week on the *Multifamily Investor Nation*. We wrote this whole book. And there's still always more to learn.

There's nothing wrong with investing with a new operator, as long as they have gained experience in the business by partnering with another operating group in order to learn the ropes. You wouldn't want to invest with someone who just went to a conference and got a bright idea. As a matter of fact, I'd rather invest with a first-time operator who is transparent about being new and about their past joint ventures, than with someone who claims to hold 1,000 units but is really only a passive investor in 1,000 units. It's not the same thing at all.

One way to assess an operator's level of experience and understanding is to simply ask them questions about the offering documents and the deal structure—especially anything you may find confusing, incomplete, or unclear. Ask them to walk you through the waterfall—dollars in, dollars out, where is it all going? If the operator can't explain their own deal in a way that you can understand, you have to wonder how well they understand it themselves. It calls into question whether they put together the deal structure thoughtfully and strategically, or are just using templates and boilerplate from their lawyer or real estate coach.

After experience, you want to vet them on performance. Were the deals they participated in successful? Did they make money for the investors, or only for themselves? Worse yet, did anyone involved lose money? You need to see real-world results.

Now, how do you know that an operator actually has the experience and accomplishments that they claim? There's a lot of smoke and mirrors out there, and you need to be able to trust your partner. The best way to verify their claims is to ask them for a track record of their past deals, and then follow up by asking about their partners and investors. Talk to some of the people who have invested with them in the past. That can give you great insight into their performance and their reliability.

Red Flags of Bad Operators

As I mentioned earlier, I started in the multifamily sector as a passive investor myself, and I still invest passively with many different operating groups as well as into my own projects. My wife and I are passively invested in a lot of syndications across the Carolinas, Georgia, Tennessee, Florida, Idaho, Maryland, Virginia, Arkansas, Indiana, and Texas. We are constantly on the lookout for new opportunities, and we've developed a list of personal red flags to watch out for.

When I say red flag, I mean it. These aren't yellow flags—warning signs that you should pause or investigate further. These are instant dealbreakers. If you encounter one of these red flags in an offering document or when researching an operator, close that file and move on. Don't waste another minute thinking about it because that group is a hard "no." Just press DELETE.

RED FLAG #1: NO SUCCESSFUL BUSINESS BACKGROUND

One of the sponsors of the syndication must have a successful background in business. The key word here is "successful," since I know people who know how to run a business, but they know how to run it into the ground. I think you know what I mean here. I want to invest with an operator that can successfully run a business even when times get tough like we saw in the financial crisis of 2008, the COVID-19 pandemic, and what we are seeing now in the volatile capital market.

The reason why this is important is that when we are buying a large asset of $100 million or more, it is more like we are buying a fully operational business that just so happens to have real estate attached to it. The operator must know how to manage people, put systems, procedures, and processes in place, and also be able to set proper KPIs to monitor the performance of the asset on a consistent basis.

RED FLAG #2: A PART-TIME OPERATOR

Real estate syndication is a full-time business and must be treated as such. If you aren't clear about why a sound operator must work full-time in the business, please go back and read Sections 1 through 3 of this book, and focus particularly on the discussion of roles and responsibilities in Chapter 1. That's the scope of work it takes to successfully manage a multifamily operation.

There are many people that are getting into the real estate syndication business, but also want to keep their W-2 income. I have worked hard for my money and do not want someone who is not all-in to manage my investment. This type of business cannot be run like a hobby on nights and weekends. I demand full-time efforts to watch my investments, and you should too.

RED FLAG #3: A SOLO OPERATOR

You should NEVER invest with an operator if there is only one partner. My preference is to have at least 2 unrelated partners (ideally 3 partners) on the project. I personally know of an investor who invested $200,000 of his own money and also brought in $200,000 of a friend's money, where the operator went ghost on them after 6 months. They cannot find the operator and they can't get their money back. A group of 2 or 3 unrelated managing partners going ghost on you is highly unlikely.

RED FLAG #4: NO PREFERRED RETURN OR PREFERRED RETURN WITH GP CATCH-UP

Every deal must have preferred returns for the limited partners (passive investors). The preferred returns align the partners' interests with the investors' so that the investors get the preferred distributions of cash flows. The preferred return allows the investor to receive 100% of the cash flows and sale proceeds up to a certain return amount, typically 7–10% depending on the deal. The deal could not be done without the investors. The operator should be willing to provide the preferred returns to maintain a successful relationship.

Also be sure that the operator offers a true preferred return. This means that 100% of the initial cash flows go to the passive investors and there is no GP (general partner) catch-up provision. The catch-up provisions in this state of the market are too rich for a deal and only benefit the operator, not you as a passive investor. I prefer to incentivize the operator to outperform and allow them the opportunity to have higher equity splits on the back end so I can protect my investment.

We'll go deeper into preferred returns and catchups in our discussion of deal structure below.

RED FLAG #5: PROJECTING RETURNS WITH A REFINANCE

I always prefer to review the underwriting of a deal prior to making a final decision to invest. One of the main items that I look for is whether the operator is including a refinance in the projections. I have invested in a deal with a refinance, and it has not gone as planned, with the returns being impacted greatly. I will not invest in a deal that is projecting a refinance because if the deal only makes sense with a refinance included, then it is too tight for my liking. In my book, modeling a refinance is an extremely aggressive move and sets you up for failure from the very beginning.

Most groups that I have seen that include a refinance in their projections are those that are very fee-heavy on the front end, or they are trying to include a GP catch-up provision to allow them to pull off excess cash from the deal prior to returning capital to investors. Always review the waterfall in the PPM to check for these types of sneaky add-ons.

Bottom-line on this one…if you see a refinance included in the LP return projections of a deal that you are reviewing…just stop reviewing and run the other direction. There are plenty of other deals out there that are much more conservative.

Now, don't get me wrong here. I certainly want to have a refinance in the business plan of a deal. However, I don't want it to be modeled into the projections. It should be the icing on the cake, and the success of the deal should not be dependent upon the refinance.

There's a further discussion of conservative underwriting in Chapter 6.

RED FLAG #6: DISTRIBUTIONS AS RETURN OF CAPITAL

When distributions are being made, they should be classified as return *on* capital and not return *of* capital. This is a very important distinction, and you should read your PPMs carefully to fully understand how they classify distributions.

There are many implications at play here when classifying the distributions as return of capital, including tax consequences and the reduction of the preferred return, since the preferred return calculation is based on the unreturned capital contributions. The preferred return percentage does not change, but the amount of the preferred return you receive will go down each time a distribution is made. This allows the operator to pull off cash flows faster since the preferred return amount is going down.

This is another tactic that is typically done with an operator that is not full-time in the business: they need the cash flows to live off of, or to eventually be able to quit their full-time job. In other words, this is usually only done with an under-capitalized group and you should run the other way…fast!

RED FLAG #7: NO SKIN IN THE GAME

Last but certainly not least, the operator must have skin in the game. I really like to see 10% of the equity required invested in the deal alongside the limited partners. However, some operators cannot invest that much, so at a minimum I want to see $100,000 invested from the operator. I want to make sure that the operator is making the best decisions. If they have money to lose, I can be assured they will make the best decisions for all of us in the deal.

RED FLAG #8: NO INTEREST RATE CAP

If you're looking at a deal that has a floating interest rate, make sure it has an interest rate cap. The debt market can change drastically during the holding period of a deal, and we've seen operators who didn't plan ahead wind up in dire straits because of it. Of course, higher interest rates mean lower demand and lower prices for real estate. If your operator doesn't buy a rate cap and interest rates spike, they could run out of cash and be forced into a quick sale—and they'll be selling in a down market. We've seen investors lose money in that scenario, so watch out for this red flag on any deal you're contemplating.

Your Offering Documents

Now that you've had an overview for what to look for—and what to look out for—in your offering documents, let me walk you through the type of documents you'll find in an offering package, and the main elements that can guide your decision-making. Let me preface this section by saying that I am not a lawyer, and you should review any agreements with your own attorney before you sign them.

Your lawyer may poke holes in what they see and want to negotiate changes. An operator may or may not agree to that, but in any event, you should have someone in your corner who can explain everything to you in the level of detail that you need, and ensure that you fully understand and agree with everything you're signing. That said, I am very familiar with using these documents as both an operator and an investor, so let's dive in.

What's in the Packet?

Typically, you'll get 4 sets of documents: the PPM, the Operating Agreement, the Subscription Agreement, and depending on the type of deal, you may also get an investor questionnaire. The PPM introduces you to the offering and discloses the risks and projected returns. The Operating Agreement is the document that governs the SPE that will own the asset—the voting rights, company structure, and so forth. Anyone who's owned a business entity will have used a company agreement.

The Subscription Agreement is your agreement to buy shares in the SPE from the operator. If the deal is organized under Rule 506(b) with non-accredited, sophisticated investors able to participate, then you'll find a questionnaire that goes into your experience with real estate and investments, your net worth and liquidity, and other means of verifying that you are qualified to participate in the deal.

You can find more information about Rule 506(b) and investor qualifications in Chapter 3.

All in all, it's likely to be over 100 pages. You should read the whole thing through. Don't sign blindly—why would you, especially with the amount of money you're contemplating for this investment? Go through the paperwork thoroughly and ask questions.

You should take a deep dive into that Operating Agreement so you really understand your voting rights, what decisions the investors need to be involved in (or not), and who the ultimate decision makers will be. You also need to understand how the money is being distributed. You need to know your rights and how the process will work. You need to know whether you'll receive a preferred return, and whether your distributions are structured as return of capital or return on capital.

After you sign and return the document, the operator will counter-sign and provide the wiring instructions. At that point, there's nothing more for a passive investor to do but fund the investment. After that, you'll receive your cash distributions and your tax documents on a regular basis. You can do as little or as much as you want to follow your investment and stay in touch, but your responsibilities are complete. That's why they call it passive investing.

Deal Structures

Before I look at anything else in an offering document, I go straight to the distribution schedule. I want to see that the deal offers preferred returns and how the cash flow and capital distributions are structured. Most offerings will contain at least 2 types of waterfalls on the returns: a cash flow waterfall and a capital event waterfall. If the refinance of the asset is treated differently than other capital events like a sale, there might be a third type of waterfall for the refinancing of the asset.

The cash flow waterfall determines the distribution of excess cash (net income) that comes in during the holding period. The asset produces revenue from rents and fees. The expenses get paid and the debt gets paid, and a portion of the excess cash comes back to the investors as a distribution.

The capital event waterfall governs the distribution of returns when there's a refinance, a supplemental loan, or the asset is sold. (Sometimes the sale is lumped in with other capital events, and sometimes it's treated differently, but for the purposes of this discussion, I'll put them together.) When there are proceeds from a sale or refinance, that capital needs to be returned to the investors. The waterfall structure shows who gets paid first, and how much they will receive before the next hurdle in the waterfall is activated.

WHAT'S A WATERFALL?

If these terms are new to you, your eyes might be starting to glaze over. Let me unpack this concept. When cash comes into a business, some of it goes to pay expenses and keep the operations going. After those expenses are paid, where does the net income go? For a multifamily asset, it goes back to the partners—the investors and the operator. The waterfall represents how that cash is divided among them. Depending on how much net income there is, the distribution of cash changes. Each level in the waterfall is represented by a "bucket."

As you see in the illustration, money flows into the top bucket—that might be net operating income, the proceeds of a refinance, or the proceeds of a sale—until it reaches a certain level, called a hurdle. In this case, we'll call it the preferred return hurdle. One hundred percent of the cash goes into this bucket until we reach the agreed-upon preferred return, let's say 7%. All the money in that bucket goes to the investors with a limited partner equity position.

As more money comes into the first bucket, that obligation (or hurdle) has been met, so the bucket overflows. The cash in excess of that 7% return begins flowing into the second bucket. This money will be distributed differently. Normally, it will be split between the investors and the operator in a particular ratio, like 70/30 or 80/20. The investors will get 70% of this money, and the operators will get 30%. There could be more hurdles and more changes in the split as the cash increases, or the waterfall may end here, and everything keeps getting split 70/30 to infinity.

For example, you might find a performance hurdle on that second bucket. Let's say the second hurdle is achieving an IRR of 13%. If the operator outperforms the expectations of the deal and the asset reaches a 13% IRR, then the second bucket will overflow and the excess cash will go into a third bucket with an even more favorable split, like a 50/50 ratio. At that point, the operator and the investors will each get 50% of the cash in this bucket. This incentivizes the operator to outperform.

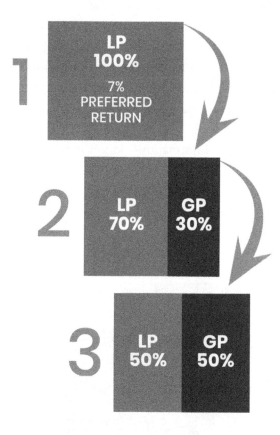

The two categories of limited partners can be broken down into classes. Class A limited partners might get higher preferred returns, which have lower risk but no upside potential upon a sale. Class B limited partners might forgo higher preferred returns in favor of a greater share of the upside as the deal outperforms expectations. Which type of shares you buy dictates your place in the waterfall. You might want to take advantage of both.

Make sure you read those sections thoroughly and understand what's happening to your money. If there's a refinance, will you get your capital returned before the operator makes a profit? Perhaps the operator will split the proceeds of a refinance with you, but pay you first from the proceeds of a sale. You need to see exactly where you fit into the structure.

There can be many different nuances to the way these waterfalls are structured, in terms of when operators qualify for fees or get a favorable split of the returns. You'll see various numbers of buckets, sizes of buckets, and ratios of equity splits. Some of these differences are just a matter of preference. Some of them I consider to be red flags that the deal isn't worth it.

You can find more information about waterfalls and equity splits in Chapter 7.

CAPITAL STACKS

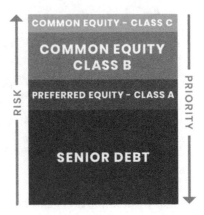

Another common way to visualize your position in a deal is as a capital stack. While waterfalls are most commonly used to describe cash flow, a capital stack describes the volume of capital, risk, and priority of returns. The thickness of each slice represents the proportion of each type of capital in the deal. The position in the stack represents the stakeholder's risk and return. The bottom of the stack has the lowest risk, and the top of the stack has the highest risk. By the same token, the bottom of the stack has the lowest returns, and the top has the highest returns.

The bottom layer is debt. The lender gets paid their interest rate, and their loan is guaranteed by a guarantor, by potentially foreclosing on the property, or both. Their risk is extremely low, and their return is secure but relatively low. It's also possible to have that layer divided into senior debt and mezzanine debt, which would be paid before the preferred equity positions.

The next layer represents limited partners, and this is where you should see your preferred and common equity shares. The LP layer might be divided into Class A and Class B, with Class B carrying more risk by not having preferred returns, but potentially taking more profit in an equity split. The top layer represents the operator and might be designated as either GP or as Class C.

When there's a capital event like a refinance or a sale, the debt gets paid off first. Then the rest of the layers are paid in ascending order: preferred equity up to their capped returns, then Class B up to their equity split, and the remainder goes to the operator.

Most of our deals offer 9% preferred returns for Class A investors, along with a preferred position in the cash flow distribution. After all our obligations are met to Class A, then Class B gets a split of cash flow and a split of the capital return. One nuance you should look out for is the proportion of Class A to Class B, because the volume of returns that need to be paid out in a preferred position make it harder to meet that obligation fully. If a deal has 40% to 50% Class A preferred equity, you wind up with very little difference in the level of risk between Class A and Class B. I'd say that 10% to 25% on the low end, to 30% or 35% on the high end, would be an optimal range for the proportion of Class A equity.

Choosing your place in the deal structure has a lot to do with choosing your lifestyle. Investors who are seeking immediate cash flow to help offset some bills or even to fund their retirement should choose a preferred position. In a preferred equity position, you'll receive consistent cash flow during the holding period as long as the property continues to perform well, but no participation in the upside of the deal at the end. This is an ideal position for someone who wants steady income with lower risk, but isn't really concerned about growth.

Investors who are willing to give up some cash flow now for a bigger pop at the end of the holding period might choose a Class B position. And of course, you could take a blended approach by investing in both Class A and Class B shares, perhaps in a 50/50 or 75/25 split. This can hedge your risk while also getting more long-term return.

You'll find more detail on preferred returns, catchups, and the capital stack in Chapter 7.

There are many different ways to structure a deal, and none of them are objectively right or wrong. The important thing to understand is how well the deal aligns with your goals.

Why Are Preferred Returns So Important?

I want to impress on you the significance of preferred returns in a deal structure. As I mentioned earlier, a lack of preferred returns is a red flag to walk away from an operator. I have never invested, and will never invest, in a deal that doesn't offer preferred returns. It's an instant dealbreaker. I don't even bother reading any further into the document.

There are several reasons (or excuses) operators give as to why they don't offer preferred returns. I'm going to debunk them for you because I don't accept them for myself, and I don't think you should accept them either.

COMPLEXITY

Some operators claim that they don't offer preferred returns because it makes the deal too complicated for their investors to understand. Now,

I don't know what kind of investors they're dealing with, but I work with some really smart—I'd say brilliant—investors. They figure this stuff out quite easily, especially when they grasp the very basic concept that the preferred return protects them. The investor comes first, and they get the firstfruits of the returns.

The preferred return isn't a guarantee because nobody can guarantee the results of an investment. But there is an obligation that whatever cash flow the investment brings, the preferred returns get paid before the operator equity splits kick in. Unless the deal fails completely, you will get your money back, and you will get the return you expected. And if you choose a well-planned deal with a reliable operator, the risk of the deal completely tanking is very low.

ALIGNMENT

I've heard some operators who don't offer preferred returns claim that this structure aligns their interests with the investors. I can't even explain the reasoning on this one because it just doesn't make any sense. Let's say you have a deal without a preferred return, with a 70/30 split. If the deal underperforms because of a market downturn or some other reason, then your 70% isn't worth anything. You'll get your initial capital back, but no return on that investment at all. Meanwhile, the operator got an interest-free loan for 5 years. How is that alignment?

No, *having* a preferred return aligns the operator with your best interest. If the operator is obligated to pay you first before they get paid, they will work very hard and make strategic decisions (like holding the asset through a market downturn) so that they can get the biggest returns they can. They don't get paid until you get paid. That's alignment.

PARI PASSU

This structure can be a little sneaky because the deal appears to offer a preferred return. But it isn't a true preferred return. This type of deal is sometimes called a **GP catch-up** provision. In the waterfall structure, there's an extra bucket between the preferred return and the first equity split. After the preferred return is met, all the cash starts flowing to the operator, and none to the investors. The hurdle for this bucket is that the operator will receive all the cash *as if they had had a 30% split all along*, and the investors don't get another dime until the operator is "caught up." This type of structure can really eat into the investors' profits, because in most cases the operator is not hitting the equity splits until after the preferred return is paid during a sale of the asset. Now the operator has to catch themselves up for several years' worth of lagging equity splits due to the GP preferred return catch-up provision. This is too rich for most deals and really eats into the profits for the passive investors.

Deals with a pari passu provision tend to have a lot of creative underwriting going on to make the numbers work. You'll see overprojected rent premiums, underprojected expenses, or underwriting for a refinance when a refinance doesn't really make sense. They may also have some creative marketing. Sometimes I'll ask an operator whether they have a GP catchup and they'll say no, but when I read the offering memorandum, it's right there. There are enough nuances with the different types of waterfalls, and the different terms used, that some operators will claim they misunderstood the question.

Just say no to GP catchup or pari passu structures. They're expensive, and they tend to come with a lot of baggage that you don't want in a passive investment.

INCOME

Another reason you might hear from an operator failing to offer preferred returns is that having an immediate income stream allows them to focus completely on the deal. This generally means that they are hoping to subsist on that cash flow, or else they'll need to keep working their "day job." That's a red flag about the operator on several levels.

As I said before, I don't recommend investing with any operator who isn't already working full-time in their syndication business because doing it correctly is a full-time job. They need a team working with them, and no distractions from managing your asset. They should not need that cash flow to put food on the table.

Next, if they are subsisting on the cash flow, they are probably too undercapitalized to have invested in the deal themselves. They have no skin in the game. Furthermore, the operator should receive asset management fees for their day-to-day management of the project. That's how they get paid for the work they do and how they pay their employees. If they aren't getting asset management fees, they probably didn't structure the deal very well. If those fees aren't sufficient to keep their business team going, then they aren't running that business effectively.

When you read through your offering documents, make sure that true preferred returns are the foundation of the deal structure. Failure to offer a preferred return is connected to many other potential problems with the operator and the deal structure. For the savvy passive investor, they aren't just a preference—they're a requirement.

The Best Choices Are Educated Choices

When you've planned a strong overall strategy and chosen the right operators and the right deals, you should expect your wealth to grow. You need to be prepared for that growth. In the final chapter, we'll cover your options for legacy wealth building and powerful tax strategies to make the most of your passive investments.

Chapter 14

Building Wealth with Multifamily Investing

Dan Handford

There's a lot to love about multifamily investing. If you ask most investors what they like best about multifamily, they'll probably mention cash flow. That's a great aspect, but my favorite benefit of this sector is the tax benefits that come along with commercial real estate investing. There's always some kind of hubbub in the news about what this or that administration might do about tax policy, but at the end of the day, Democrats and Republicans both invest in commercial real estate, and they aren't going to shoot themselves in the foot. Not too much, anyway. There are many advantages for commercial real estate investors built into the tax code that allow you to keep more of the returns on your investments.

In this chapter, I'll cover legacy wealth building and the tax benefits available to passive multifamily investors, such as investing through your IRA and using Deferred Sales Trusts and the Delaware Statutory Trust (DSTs). I'll also go over how you can reduce your tax bills through depreciation, cost segregation, and the power of the 1031 Like-Kind Exchange.

Tax Advantages of Passive Investing

Before I delve into the tax strategies that you need to understand, I want to make something perfectly clear. When I talk about deferring, offsetting, or avoiding taxes, I'm not talking about trying to *cheat* on your taxes. We don't try to skirt the IRS. We pay every penny of taxes that we owe. But we don't pay taxes that we don't owe, and we don't pay them years or decades before they're really due.

Every topic in this chapter is a legal provision built into the tax code. They are designed to benefit real estate investors, because real estate investment is good for the economy and for the communities where investment is happening. For you as the investor, tax offsets and tax deferrals allow you to grow the capital you have available to invest. The more you invest, the more you can diversify, and the more gains you can achieve to accelerate your wealth building. With that, let's look at some of the incredible tools the law provides to incentivize your investments.

Depreciation and Cost Segregation

One of the biggest advantages we have as passive investors is depreciation. No matter what asset class or asset size you invest in, depreciation is available to you. Many new investors aren't aware of this concept and the difference it makes in your bottom line.

Depreciation is just as important to your long-term wealth strategy as the appreciation of your assets or your cash flow. Depreciation is a way of accounting for the wear and tear on a property over time. On paper, the asset's value decreases every year, and you can take that loss as a deduction on your taxable income. Depreciation is so powerful for passive investors because it can be used to offset passive income from other sources as well. I have investors who invest with us just to get that depreciation. Better yet, if you can't use all the depreciation in 1 year because you didn't have enough passive income, you can carry it forward to use in the future.

Now, you may be familiar with depreciation on an asset like a house. The value of the house is depreciated over 27 and a half years, and each year you can deduct a portion of that "loss" according to a predetermined schedule. That's known as straight-line depreciation. There are 2 other types of depreciation available to commercial real estate investors: accelerated depreciation and bonus depreciation.

Accelerated depreciation allows you to depreciate parts of the asset more quickly than the whole, so you can take most of the depreciation in a short holding period instead of waiting the full 27 and a half years. In order to apply accelerated depreciation, the operator needs to employ cost segregation analysis.

Here's how cost segregation works: multifamily communities aren't uniform buildings that depreciate on a single fixed schedule. In reality, different pieces of the property are going to wear out and lose value at different rates. The stoves in the apartments might depreciate in 4 years and the countertops in 10 years. Cost segregation itemizes the different pieces of the asset into separate depreciation schedules, so your annual tax deduction reflects the real life span of the items within the property.

A third-party engineer analyzes the property, taking into account the vintage, the upgrades, and the features of the individual units. They then calculate a new depreciation schedule based on the life spans of those disparate parts. This allows us to accelerate the depreciation of the asset by front-loading those costs into the first 5 years of the holding period.

Bonus depreciation is a temporary measure that Congress enacts from time to time as an economic stimulus. It allows commercial property owners to take extra depreciation on renovations they make early in the holding period. At the time of this writing, we're benefitting from the strongest bonus depreciation that's ever been on the books: 100% depreciation capital expenditures to improve the property in the first year of ownership. That's huge. The same level of bonus depreciation may or may not be available at the time you read this book, because it's an incentive that gets changed up pretty regularly. You should certainly ask your operator whether they take advantage of it, and your tax advisor on how best to apply it to your own tax situation.

I'm covering a lot of technical jargon here, and many passive investors aren't that interested in geeking out over the technicalities. They just want to know how it impacts them. I understand! For those readers, let's cut to the chase: if you invest $100,000 in a multifamily deal with straight line depreciation, accelerated depreciation, and bonus depreciation, you could potentially take $50,000 to $70,000 in depreciation benefit in year 1, even if you're getting income from the property. For every dollar you put in, you're getting half of it back as depreciation. For high income earners, that's a very, very powerful tool to reduce your tax burden.

On the flip side, those taxes will come due eventually. Depreciation lowers your taxable income, but it raises your capital gains when the asset gets sold. Some people (and even some operators) downplay the value of depreciation because the taxes are deferred instead of eliminated. That's shortsighted. By reducing your tax bills now, you have more money in your pocket to reinvest in another project. Then you can compound your returns by deploying your capital widely and diversifying your portfolio.

The most straightforward method of using depreciation to reduce your taxes is to immediately acquire more properties! When you take a gain from selling a property, and buy another property in the same year, the depreciation from the new property can help to offset your gain from the sale (if not all the gain, probably most of it). You're balancing your gain with an immediate loss. It's simplistic, but it's worked out very well for us over the years.

You'll find a detailed discussion of depreciation and capital gains tax in Chapter 10.

Cost segregation and bonus depreciation (if available) are such important tax benefits, you should consider them dealbreakers. I'd seriously question any operator who isn't using depreciation to your advantage as an investor. They're either naive to the tax laws, or they're unsophisticated in their long-term strategy. Either way, that's a big red flag not to invest with them. There's one important exception to that rule: if the operator only accepts investments through self-directed IRAs, there's no tax advantage to using cost segregation, because you're already tax-free. In any event, most operators have a relatively small percentage of IRA funds. They should plan the deal to be favorable to all their investors.

1031 Like-Kind Exchange

The 1031 exchange is a tax deferral strategy that was born in the 1920s, almost as soon as the IRS began. Legislators realized that allowing owners to exchange assets without paying taxes every time would keep money moving in the economy, rather than having people park their money and do nothing with it. Owners have more money in their pockets to renovate and improve their assets, which also benefits residents and the community as a whole. This tax incentive motivates people to make things better.

Here's how it works. If you're accumulating investment property, taking the cash flow, using the depreciation, and appreciating the value of the asset, at some point you'll be ready to sell that asset and trade up. You bought the asset for $100,000, and you can now sell it for $200,000.

Ordinarily, you'd owe capital gains tax on that $100,000 gain. However, the 1031 provision allows you to defer those taxes and trade up to another asset that's equal or better in value. So all that gain can be put to work in a new investment. The capital gains tax doesn't come due until you cash out of a 1031 and receive the gain. As long as you keep rolling over the value of one asset to another, you can defer that tax. It's even possible to defer those capital gains taxes for the rest of your life, as long as you keep the chain of 1031s going. When you die, your heirs will receive the property at its current value, and they won't owe taxes on those gains either. All that growth was tax-free.

Now, that's an oversimplification to some extent. There are always nuances and special circumstances to take into consideration, but that's the high-level view. Rolling a 1031 exchange into an apartment syndication, or rolling your share of a sale into a 1031 takes some extra paperwork and a knowledgeable operator to accommodate you. Not all operators will work with 1031s, because it creates an extra step in the process. But it's a really valuable tool, especially in hot markets where asset values can jump 20% or 30% in just a couple of years. That produces massive capital gains. If building long-term wealth is your goal, look for an operator who can help you with a 1031.

You can find a more detailed discussion of capital gains and 1031 exchanges in Chapter 10.

DSTs (Both Kinds)

The term DST can refer to 2 entirely separate instruments: Delaware Statutory Trusts or Deferred Sales Trusts. The 2 structures are unrelated, and the acronyms are just a really unfortunate coincidence. Both types of trusts can be used to defer tax on the proceeds of an asset sale, but they work differently.

DELAWARE STATUTORY TRUSTS

Normally, if you're investing in an apartment syndication via a 1031 exchange, you would need to do that within a Tenancy in Common (TIC) structure, which the operator would arrange (hence the extra paperwork). An alternative to investing in a TIC would be to place the proceeds of that 1031 exchange into a Delaware Statutory Trust. There are companies that sponsor DSTs and pool funds from 1031 investors to purchase multifamily assets.

Operators who can accommodate 1031 investments often have higher minimums for 1031 investors than for limited partners who invest with cash because of the additional work involved in setting up a TIC structure. At PassiveInvesting.com, our minimum for 1031 funds is $1 million. For investors who have smaller amounts of capital available, we recommend that they use a DST instead. Minimum investments in a DST are typically in the range of $50,000 to $100,000.

The main caveat with using a DST is that they're often heavily fee-driven. They use a broker dealer who takes a fee off the top, usually 6% to 10%. So for a $100,000 investment, you'd have to put in $106,000 to $110,000 in order to meet the minimum.

In addition, the sponsor of a DST is legally barred from owning any portion of the trust. They act solely as a trustee, and they can't receive any equity splits. This is supposed to keep the trustee independent, but you lose the alignment of interest that is so beneficial with a typical general partner. The DST will have higher acquisition fees, higher asset management fees, and higher exit fees, because it's the only way they can make money.

DEFERRED SALES TRUSTS

This structure is a form of installment sale when you sell a property that allows you to defer capital gains tax when you can't use a 1031 exchange. Before the sale, you transfer the property into the trust. The trust sells the property on your behalf and holds the proceeds. The trust then pays you in installments over time.

There are 2 ways to arrange these payments. You could receive the proceeds of the sale, which would be subject to capital gains tax, but the installments would spread out your tax burden over multiple years. Or you could have the trust invest the proceeds into a new property and pay you from the dividends of that investment. Then you wouldn't receive any capital gains, and therefore you'd owe no capital gains tax.

As with every kind of tax topic, there are always layers of nuance and exceptions or special considerations. However, both types of DSTs can be very effective alternatives to a 1031 exchange.

Real Estate Professional Status

We discussed the real estate professional status extensively in Chapter 10, with a focus on operators. But you don't have to become an operator in order to claim this status. Let me explain.

Real estate professional status makes your depreciation into an even greater tax benefit. As a passive investor, you can only offset passive income with passive depreciation. However, a real estate professional can use that depreciation to offset all income from any source. You don't need any type of professional license or certification to be qualified as a real estate professional for tax purposes. The requirements are that you spend at least 750 hours a year working in the industry, and at least 51% of your working hours in a real estate related position.

A real estate related position doesn't mean becoming a real estate agent. It could mean managing your portfolio of real estate investments, overseeing your rental properties, attending conferences, and pursuing your education about the industry. If you have a regular job that you love, 750 hours can be too much to take on.

However, there's a great opportunity available for married couples who file jointly. If your spouse isn't already working full-time, they could put in the hours to qualify for professional status. Then your joint deduction for depreciation can offset your joint income, even the earned income from your professional job.

If you decide to take advantage of this option, make sure you discuss it thoroughly with your CPA first. You must also document all your hours impeccably. Real estate professional status can be a magnet for IRS audits, and you don't want to have anything incomplete or incorrect.

There are smart choices you can make about applying depreciation, as well. If you don't have much in the way of gains one year, you could carry forward a significant offset. Perhaps you plan to sell an asset the following year—that's the right time to apply that depreciation. If you have a good CPA, they can walk you through all your options.

Grow Your Knowledge, Grow Your Wealth

As you can see, a tax-savvy approach to investing can be rocket fuel for your net worth. Whether you're contemplating your first passive multifamily investment, or hoping to improve your results, understanding your tax options is one of the smartest moves you can make.

Educating yourself about your financial future is the best investment you can make with your time. Don't just turn off your brain and watch Netflix. Go learn how to leverage your portfolio and your tax benefits to your best advantage. As a matter of fact, I hope you learn something from every chapter of this book that will bring you one step closer to the future you want for yourself and your family.

Conclusion

Welcome!

Now that you've read and absorbed this book, we're pleased to welcome you into the apartment syndication business and the world of opportunity it provides. By investing the time to learn about this business, you've already begun your journey to greater freedom and personal control of your financial future.

We're passionate about multifamily investing because it combines some of the most powerful benefits an investor can find: immediate cash flow, the ability to increase the value of your asset through smart planning and hard work, and the tax benefits that help you build long-term wealth. We're excited to share those insights with you, to encourage and equip you as you grow and diversify your portfolio with well-chosen real estate assets.

We've covered a lot of ground together. Back in Part 1, we stressed the importance of understanding the language of multifamily investing. We hope you're keeping notes so you can refer back to these terms when you read offering documents or pursue further learning opportunities. We also introduced you to the basic structure of syndications, the roles of active and passive investors, and the many different skill sets needed to run a successful multifamily operation. Launching and maintaining your own operating group brings with it a big responsibility to your investors. Fulfilling that responsibility is a full-time job.

You also learned all the reasons why large apartment communities are such an excellent investment, strategies to begin passive investing at different financial levels, and how a successful operator grows and communicates with their investor network.

In Part 2, we drilled down on setting your investment criteria, analyzing markets, and analyzing individual properties to find the ones that will be profitable. We covered how multifamily lending works, and broke down the structure of multifamily deals so you can choose the risk and returns that are right for you. We also walked you through the timeline of a multifamily acquisition, so both active and passive investors can know what to expect.

Part 3 focused on the day-to-day operations of running a multifamily business, both in terms of managing the physical asset and making sure the financial asset is profitable. Whether you're managing the property manager, choosing the right time to sell, or planning your tax strategy, sound management is key to your success as an operator.

In Part 4, we took the perspective of a passive investor. You learned how to set your overall investing strategy and use multifamily deals to diversify your portfolio. We showed you how to choose the right operators to invest with and how to recognize those you should definitely *not*. Finally, we delved into advanced investing strategies for maximizing your tax benefits and creating a legacy for future generations.

We hope this book has allowed you to get to know us, come to like us, and that we've earned your trust. We see this book as an important part of building our relationship with you and other investors new to the multifamily sector. We hope you'll use every part of this book to take the next step forward in your investing journey.

Don't stop here! We've grown our business from nothing to billions in our portfolio, and we're still learning how to improve all the time. If you want exponential growth, you have to keep learning, too. There are any number of experts and veteran operators out there who have different perspectives and valuable insight to share. We have our own philosophy about the industry, and you've had a taste of it in this book. If you think our approach is a good fit for you, please join us at MultifamilyInvestorNation.com to keep the conversation going.

If you're ready to see specific investment opportunities and find the right deal for your next passive investment, you can become a member of our Passive Investor Club at PassiveInvesting.com. Joining the club will place you in our investor network so you can receive all the insider information about our business and our upcoming projects.

Above all, if you found this book valuable, we hope you'll share it with someone else. That's the highest compliment we could possibly receive.

If you take nothing else from this book, we hope you understand the amazing potential of multifamily investing to change your financial outlook, your lifestyle, and your legacy. Our investor Sally was able to overcome her money worries and spend precious time with her son. We see investors every day who have been able to create the life they really want, retire early, and create security for their families. We are so grateful to be part of their stories.

Today you get to choose—what will your story be?

Made in the USA
Las Vegas, NV
01 November 2023

80053871R00144